Coping with
Schizophrenia

A guide for patients, families and caregivers

Steven Jones and Peter Hayward

ONEWORLD
OXFORD

COPING WITH SCHIZOPHRENIA

Oneworld Publications
(Sales and Editorial)
185 Banbury Road
Oxford OX2 7AR
England
www.oneworld-publications.com

ISBN 1-85168-344-5

Cover design by Mungo Designs
Typeset by Pracharak, India
Printed and bound in the US by McNaughton & Gunn

Contents

Acknowledgements

This book was inspired by our clinical work with people who have a diagnosis of schizophrenia and their families. We have also been involved in research into both the psychological factors associated with this disorder and the development of psychological treatments. Over the last ten to fifteen years there have been numerous studies which have indicated the important role that psychological and social interventions can have for people with a diagnosis of schizophrenia. The work of psychological research groups in Manchester, London and elsewhere led the British Government to highlight the importance of access to psychological treatment for people with schizophrenia in its National Service Framework. The work of user groups has also provided important evidence of the valued role that people with this diagnosis can have, even in the presence of ongoing symptoms. This is important in demonstrating that improvement or recovery is not based solely on the removal or suppression of diagnostic symptoms but on the development and maintenance of valued roles and activities.

Although there have been positive developments for people with this diagnosis, our experience is still that many people with this diagnosis, and their families, often have access to very little relevant information. Many people are unsure what a diagnosis of schizophrenia might mean and what the implications of this for their future lives might be. The intention of this book is to provide information in an accessible form concerning a wide range of issues related to living with a diagnosis of schizophrenia. The hope is that this information will be a useful part of helping people to be active agents with respect to their own care, both medical and psychological.

We also want to mention people who have advised us on specific chapters, such as Elizabeth Kuipers, Robin Forman and Larry Rifkin. They have been generous and helpful, and hopefully any mistakes of ours have not undone their good work. Finally, we would like to thank the many sufferers with whom we have worked over the years. They have taught us a great deal; we only hope that we have been able to be as helpful to them.

1

Is this book for you?

Schizophrenia: What's in a name?

To be told that you or someone you love has a serious illness must be one of the most frightening experiences in life. 'You have cancer ... Your wife has Alzheimer's disease ... Your son has Multiple Sclerosis.' These sentences suggest death or serious disability, and no one would wish to hear them. This book is devoted to discussing the implications of an equally serious diagnosis: schizophrenia. We know from clinical experience that being told that you or a friend or relative has schizophrenia is a very frightening and confusing experience, perhaps in many cases much more frightening and confusing than with many other illnesses. Why should this be?

First of all, most people know very little about serious mental illness. Perhaps one per cent of the population is diagnosed as having schizophrenia, and other serious mental illnesses like bipolar disorder are also just as common, but the general public knows very little about them. Even in professional circles, the diagnosis of schizophrenia is surrounded with controversy, as we hope to explain. In addition, some sufferers reject the diagnosis and do not accept that it applies to them, and sometimes this is true of their caregivers as well. This rejection can occur for many reasons, but can include misconceptions about what such a diagnosis means and what its implications are. This can result in a great deal of confusion – confusion that we hope this book will help to dispel.

Is this book for you?

We wrote this book in the first instance for *sufferers*. If you are a sufferer, you have probably had a variety of odd and distressing experiences, for example hearing voices that others can't hear, believing things that other people don't accept or feeling that strangers are intruding into your life in odd and uncanny ways. In addition to this, you may find that other people are frightened of you or don't understand you, and that you have been diagnosed with what sounds like a frightening illness. We hope in this book to help you to understand more about what is happening to you, and, more importantly, to show you what you can do about it.

We have also written this book for *family members and caregivers*. If you live with or are taking care of someone with a diagnosis of schizophrenia, this can be a very difficult and burdening experience. Our aim is for this book to give hope and show that there are many things that can make your loved one's life better.

'But there's nothing wrong with me!' There is another group of people who we think might find this book helpful: those who for whatever reason have received a diagnosis of schizophrenia but don't accept it. As we hope to show, there are a fair number of people in this category. Some people may have strange and troubling experiences but feel that they cannot accept being labelled with an illness; some may find the label troubling or

unhelpful; and some may in fact, for a variety of reasons, have been wrongly diagnosed. In any case, to have received a frightening diagnosis is an unpleasant experience, and we hope that this book will help you to understand what that diagnosis means and doesn't mean. We also feel that, whether or not you accept that you have an illness, many kinds of help and support might be available, and you might choose to take advantage of some of them.

As we have already indicated, most people diagnosed with schizophrenia have a variety of strange experiences, such as hearing or feeling things that other people don't hear or feel. The general term used to describe such experiences is psychosis, or psychotic experiences. Some sufferers find this term insulting; they feel that doctors and professionals are suggesting that their experiences aren't 'really real'. This is an important subject, and we would like to make our views on it clear in the following section.

Psychotic experiences – what is reality anyway?

The title of this section may seem a bit strange, but we believe that it goes to the heart of what makes psychotic experiences so troubling for those who have them and for those who don't. Both of us, in our work, have had the same conversation many times with many patients. If patients come to see a clinical psychologist, they usually believe, in some sense, that they have a problem. Often they may go further and say that they have some sort of illness. However, asked about the reality of their experiences, for example the voices they hear or the strange ideas they have, they will reply, 'They're real.' Imagine for example a man who hears the voices of criminals threatening him, saying that they are going to kidnap him, torture him and finally kill him, and that perhaps they are going to do the same thing to his family. To have such experiences, and to believe the threat is real, must be terrifying. One might well think, 'Wouldn't a person prefer to believe that these voices are in his or her own head? After all, that would remove the threat.' But in our experience, most people with such experiences do not find such ideas either comforting or acceptable; their answer is, 'It's real.' Why might this be?

As you read these words, you are probably sitting on a chair in a room. Imagine that someone came to you and told you that you were not in a room at all, that you were really floating on an iceberg in the middle of the Arctic Ocean? You would undoubtedly think that this was a ridiculous idea. If a doctor, especially one you did not know very well, told you this, and told you further that you needed to take some medication because you thought you were sitting in a chair, you would certainly believe her to be incompetent. Even if all your friends and family swore that this was the case, you would be bound to continue to doubt it. Most people who hear voices describe their experience of those voices as being as real as the chair you are sitting in.

But how can a voice be real if there is no one speaking? This might seem to some people a watertight argument, but not everyone would agree. Many religious people believe that God can talk to people, and some think that the Devil or angels can also. People from some parts of the world have been taught from their youth that some people have magical powers, powers called, for example, voodoo or obeah: perhaps these voices have a supernatural cause. We also know that modern science is advancing all the time, and that governments and secret services may have access to technologies of which the rest of us have not heard. Do you know for a fact that MI5 or the CIA does not have a machine that can project the human voice over great distances? Perhaps these ideas might seem far-fetched to you, but we also know that the idea of a powerful electronic computer that can sit in the palm of your hand and yet gather information from around the world would have seemed pretty far-fetched as little as twenty years ago.

The point of this discussion is that most of us are seldom, if ever, asked to question the reality of our own experiences. We may disagree about things like politics or current events, but we agree with others about what is real and what is not, and we do not usually have experiences that others find strange or unbelievable. Even if we might have had fleeting experiences which might have been strange or unusual, they will not have been sufficiently intense or frequent to impact on the routine of our daily lives.

Often groups of people with unusual beliefs gather into small groups so that they can reinforce one another's beliefs. For example, in some churches, unusual experiences, such as speaking in tongues or falling suddenly into a fit, are accepted as normal and viewed as evidence of powerful religious faith. Outsiders might find this 'mad', but for the members of the church, this is normal and acceptable. And indeed, they are entitled to say to outsiders, 'You have never had these experiences, so you are not in a position to judge them. And you certainly can't produce any evidence that they are not the result of God or the Holy Spirit.' Some things cannot be tested or proved scientifically. In that sense, someone suffering from schizophrenia or another psychotic disorder is like a member of a church of one; he or she has unusual experiences of great personal significance but has no one to share them with.

One point about these experiences remains to be looked at: while most religious people find their beliefs comforting and encouraging, many psychotic experiences are deeply unpleasant, demoralising and frightening. Later in this book we will talk more about these experiences and the kind of suffering they can cause. Even though many of them are so unpleasant, many sufferers continue to believe that they are real, and some sufferers also find value in positive aspects of their experiences. In any event, they are often not helped by being told that what they experience is 'not real'. As therapists, we tend to avoid arguing with patients: we cannot tell them what they are experiencing, and, whatever we think of the causes of these experiences, we have to accept that, at least to the sufferer, they are real. Instead, we try to focus on finding ways of reducing distress, as well as helping the sufferer to understand that the experiences may be real to them, but are not real to most people. Perhaps the most helpful stance is to 'agree to differ'. It is also worth acknowledging at this point that for many people the key issue is not so much the experience of hearing voices or unusual beliefs: it is often the interpretation of these experiences and the fear or distress that this can cause which has the most profound effects on people's lives.

Help is available

So far we have explained who we are writing for and mentioned some of the factors that make schizophrenia such a difficult and confusing topic. But there is a final and most important point: a great deal of help is available to sufferers, and this book is designed to help them take advantage of it. The evidence shows that a diagnosis of schizophrenia does not necessarily condemn a sufferer to a lifetime of disability. Instead, the prognosis for sufferers is extremely variable. In addition, there are now a wide variety of treatments, including medical, psychological and psychosocial approaches, and new treatments continue to be developed. We also know that with almost any illness or problem, maintaining a positive attitude is very important, so a major goal of this book is to reinforce a sense of hope and optimism in sufferers and their caregivers.

What this book covers

Chapter 2 provides a basic introduction to the facts about schizophrenia in so far as we understand them. We discuss how common this diagnosis is and review what is known about the causes and course of the illness. Chapter 3 considers how schizophrenia is diagnosed. We also introduce a number of case histories that illustrate some of the different symptoms, treatments and effects of schizophrenia; these case histories are continued throughout the book. Chapter 4 discusses some of the frightening and misleading ideas that are commonly held about schizophrenia. Chapter 5 talks about the role of other people, both professional and non-professional, and what sort of help or support they might be able to provide. Chapter 6 discusses the various medications that are prescribed for sufferers, focusing on both benefits and side effects, while chapter 7 talks about the new developments in psychological therapies. In chapter 8 we discuss the role of self-help and how other sufferers can offer very helpful support. In chapter 9 we discuss employment, while chapter 10 is devoted to the impact of schizophrenia on families. Finally, chapter 11 looks at some of schizophrenia's long-term emotional and practical consequences.

We do not seek to minimise the difficulties that many sufferers experience, but we believe that with the right help and advice many of them can improve their situations. We have both worked for many years with sufferers of serious mental illness, and we know how difficult and discouraging many sufferers find their illnesses to be, but we have also seen many sufferers make amazing progress in their own lives, and we hope that this book will contribute, in a small way, to helping our readers do the same.

2

How common is schizophrenia and how does it affect people's lives?

This book is for people who have received a diagnosis of schizophrenia. It will also be of interest to people who know someone with this diagnosis and who want to learn more about it. However, it is not the purpose of this book to convince people to agree with this diagnosis; we know that because many people do not. However, people are usually given this diagnosis because they have particular types of problems in their lives. Our main aim is to provide useful information on how such problems might be addressed, whether or not you agree with the diagnostic label of schizophrenia. Our view is that people with mental health problems who take an active role in their own treatment often have better outcomes. People who are well informed about their diagnosis and its implications are better able to take such an active role.

Schizophrenia is not uncommon

Schizophrenia is a term that can be frightening to some people. As is discussed in more detail in chapter 4, the term can be associated with many negative stereotypes, partly as a result of portrayals in the national press. In addition, from the way it is publicly reported it can appear to be a devastating and rare disorder. This is, however, not the case. Although the consequences of schizophrenia can be very severe, this is by no means always the case. Furthermore, there has been extensive research assessing how common a diagnosis of schizophrenia is. Studies indicate that schizophrenia is a common problem. Most reports agree that there is around a one per cent prevalence rate. This means that, on average, one in every hundred people would be expected to suffer from schizophrenia. This is probably an underestimate; as such figures are usually based on people in contact with mental health services. Those people who are managing well, or who are not in contact with such services, would not be counted in such surveys. There are also many people who may experience some, but not all, of the symptoms of schizophrenia. Therefore many more than one in a hundred people have had experiences relevant to this disorder. Far from being a rare diagnosis, many people will come into contact with someone in their family or circle of friends who has had this diagnosis.

Kraepelin was wrong!

Schizophrenia can occur at any time but is usually diagnosed in late adolescence or early adulthood. It seems to occur when people are beginning to move towards adult life and living independently from their families. For a long time it was thought that people with this diagnosis were doomed to do very poorly in life. In fact, Kraepelin, the psychiatrist who first observed the symptoms of schizophrenia (then called *dementia praecox*), stated that it was marked by a chronic deteriorating course. He believed that following diagnosis people did not recover and that the vast majority became more unwell as time went on.

Even though other psychiatrists were by no means unanimous in sharing this view, it persisted for many years. In contrast to this, Bleuler, another founding father of modern psychiatry, strongly held that people often experience remission and recovery from this disorder. Although he was an influential figure, his conclusions about the possibilities for improvement and recovery from schizophrenia held less sway than Kraepelin's more pessimistic account.

However, there have been numerous studies in recent years which have collected information on what happens to people with schizophrenia in the years following their diagnosis. These recent studies have indicated that more than fifty per cent of people with schizophrenia do well. They either experience one episode with no further recurrences or they have several episodes but are able to function normally in between these. Around one in three appear to experience repeated episodes with difficulties in between these.

Thus, many people cope well with living with this diagnosis. Those people who have ongoing difficulties can still live valued lives and benefit from psychological and social, as well as pharmacological, support. Current evidence does not support a Kraepelinian approach in which recovery is impossible and the course usually worsens over time. Our intention is to provide people with information which is relevant and helpful, so that they can be active in influencing decisions about their care. This should help each individual to have a degree of control over their experiences and help towards each person achieving their best outcome.

The continuum approach

This book refers to schizophrenia, but we do not see people with this diagnosis as fundamentally different from anyone else. Rather, we have taken the continuum approach, which is common currency in clinical psychology. This approach is based on the idea that we all have some tendency towards schizophrenia (or indeed any other mental health problem). The strength of this tendency will depend on a number of factors and will vary from person to person. These factors include:

1. Basic personality. Although we are influenced by many things in our lives as we develop, research indicates that there are a number of relatively stable personality types. This does not mean that a personality dictates everything about how we behave. Rather, it acts as a filter through which life experiences pass. Thus, someone who is naturally quiet and reserved might enjoy a job which involved a significant amount of working alone, whereas a very outgoing person might find exactly the same job stressful and lonely.

2. Experiences that people have had. Many people with a diagnosis of schizophrenia will have had difficult experiences in the past; these may include relationship problems or frightening or negative events that have happened.

3. How they deal with these experiences. Many people with schizophrenia have had a range of traumatic experiences. This is also true of many people with other mental health problems and also of some people with no mental health diagnosis. The particular ways in which people react to and deal with their experiences are therefore probably associated with how they cope and the impact it has on mental health.

4. How other people react to them. Individual coping skills and approaches are of course only part of the story. None of us function in isolation and the reactions of other people to our behaviour can be very important. If people have close and supportive relationships with key figures in their lives, they tend to have better outcomes than people who do not.

Therefore, the impact of experiences is also associated with relationships and support from friends and family.

Most of us move up and down this continuum at different points in our lives, depending on all of the above factors, which can change over time. If someone has a tendency towards developing schizophrenia this does not mean that they will inevitably do so. In fact, if life goes relatively smoothly this may be no more than an element of their personality (just like sociability or self-confidence, which also vary throughout the population). However, in the presence of repeated adversity the individual can move up this continuum and potentially reach a point at which schizophrenia is diagnosed. Even then, it remains perfectly possible to move back down the continuum, particularly if people receive the right balance of medical, psychological and social help for their specific circumstances.

Although this view has been controversial in the past, there is now substantial scientific support for it. Many studies have identified schizophrenic-like (schizotypal) characteristics in the general population. Healthy individuals, who report schizotypal experiences, appear to behave in a similar manner to people with a clinical diagnosis of schizophrenia, on a whole range of tests of thinking, attitudes and beliefs. This overlap supports our view that people with this diagnosis are clearly able to benefit from approaches that help them to address their problems in living. Just like people with any other emotional problem, when people with a diagnosis of schizophrenia are able to feel happier, more secure, less frightened, more positive and more in control they do better generally. The ways in which people can achieve this can be through formal and informal support, psychological therapy and changing life circumstances. There are things that you can do; receipt of this diagnosis does not mean that the individual needs to take a passive role in his or her future care.

Social and personal costs

It is clear that for many people schizophrenia is associated with significant social and personal costs. The onset of schizophrenia can be associated with a fracturing of important personal and family relationships. People can have careers or education disrupted or ended abruptly. Hospital admissions and the circumstances leading up to them can be experienced as traumatic. People can feel that their plans and hopes for the future have been dashed by the onset of schizophrenia. This is however only part of the picture. The social and personal costs of schizophrenia vary widely. The costs can be very high for some people, but this emphasises the importance of people having an active involvement in their own care. It is clearly the case that the things that help one person with schizophrenia do not necessarily help someone else. This can be true of medications and psychological help. Therefore, when someone is an active agent in planning their own recovery, outcomes are likely to be better. One reason for this is that people who feel involved in the care decisions that are being made tend to actively engage with the programme of care that has been agreed. Where such programmes are either imposed, or passively accepted by an individual, there is a normal tendency to feel less engaged and to resist the suggestions or treatment offered. Such findings are not unique to the mental health field. Studies in social psychology and management science also indicate a human response to resist imposed change and to engage more with changes that the individual has an investment in.

There can be a great deal of variation in how people interpret their symptoms. Where one person will find their voices very distressing, someone else might regard their voices as a benefit. Thus, some people apparently live relatively happily with the experience of voices. Professor Marius Romme (a Dutch Social Psychiatrist) asked voice hearers to contact him following a television programme in Holland. He received many contacts from people with the experience of voice hearing who had had no involvement with psychiatric services. However, when voices are interpreted as powerful, malevolent and frightening, such experiences are much harder to cope with. In these situations people will often become increasingly distressed and eventually present for help.

People who have schizophrenia

Many people with this diagnosis have experienced substantial difficulties in their lives. It can often be these difficulties which move people closer to the likelihood of experiencing a schizophrenic illness. Some of the difficulties that people experience can be associated with their contacts with mental health services. At times there can be conflicts between individuals feeling frustrated and unheard and services which can see the same people as difficult and unco-operative. Although no service is perfect, the vast majority of individuals working in mental health do so because they want to help people get on with their lives. Professionals are, through their own training and through the increasing influence of user and caregiver groups, becoming more aware of the importance of negotiating with and listening to clients' views. However, both clients and mental health professionals will at times disagree, and dealing with such disagreements with mutual respect can be key to developing positive therapeutic alliances.

Our own view is that many people with a diagnosis of schizophrenia can live less disrupted lives if they can maintain contact with mental health services. We also believe that there is a responsibility on both sides to negotiate this contact so that it is mutually respectful. Individuals need to be active agents in their own care, which means having access to information that can inform their decisions. We hope that the information in this book will help in this endeavour.

Family and friends

Family and friends are important to all of us, even if we may currently see little of them. Some people with a diagnosis of schizophrenia can have very strong and supportive family relationships that are extremely beneficial. However, this is not always the case. The experience of schizophrenia can impact beyond the individual into their immediate family and social circle. Relatives and friends may not understand what is happening to their partner, child or work colleague, or they may be very frightened by what the individual is going through. If the illness is recurrent there may be confusion or anger about why it is continuing and why apparent periods of recovery have not been sustained. Sometimes anger can then be directed at the individual with schizophrenia who is sometimes seen as lazy or self-centred for not getting well. A common source of tension can be the negative symptoms of apathy and low motivation, which can appear similar to someone 'just not trying' to the external observer. Equally, conflict can run in the other direction where service users perceive hostility where it is absent or where there are basic disagreements about the nature of the problem and the best approaches to this. This can lead to arguments and tension, which can at times make the initial symptoms worse.

Again it is important that families have access both to information and support. Although this issue is increasingly being addressed, there is still a long way to go. Too many families feel isolated and adrift, unsure of what the meaning or implications of this diagnosis are and unsure of how to help. We discuss these issues in more detail in chapter 10. Chapter 7, on psychological approaches includes a discussion of work with families.

Points covered in this chapter

➡ This book aims to provide information about issues associated with a diagnosis of schizophrenia, for people with this diagnosis and for others who want to learn more about it.

➡ We hope to be informative, whether or not you agree with schizophrenia as a diagnostic label. Even if you disagree with your diagnosis, but feel you have some of the difficulties outlined in the chapter, the book is likely to be relevant to you.

➡ Schizophrenia is not uncommon. It is diagnosed in one in a hundred people. This means that most people will come into contact with people with this diagnosis at some time or another.

➡ A diagnosis of schizophrenia does not inevitably mean a poor or deteriorating outcome for the individual. Around fifty per cent of people with a diagnosis of schizophrenia do well subsequently, either experiencing only one episode or several episodes, but with good social functioning in between these.

➡ The tendency towards schizophrenia is on a continuum throughout the whole population. This means that there are some people who are well who have many characteristics which are similar to people with a diagnosis of schizophrenia. People can move up and down this continuum depending on their experiences, coping skills and support systems.

➡ Social and personal costs of schizophrenia are variable, but can be high. Schizophrenia often occurs at vulnerable times in people's lives, often as they are beginning to try to make their way in the world. However, after the initial episode many people are able to continue to live valued lives even if some symptoms persist.

➡ People who have an active role in their own recovery tend to have better outcomes. This is an important issue which requires both effort from the individual and support from the mental health services with which they are in contact.

➥ Families as well as individuals often need information and support. As chapters 7 and 10 indicate later, in addition to information there can often be an important role for psychological interventions with both families and sufferers.

3

How is schizophrenia diagnosed and what are its symptoms?

How is schizophrenia diagnosed?

There has been much debate concerning the symptoms and diagnosis of schizophrenia over the years. When the diagnosis was first described there was a lot of variability between clinicians as to who should be given this diagnosis. However, over the last twenty years reliable systems for assessment and diagnosis have been developed. In the 1970s and 80s there was a view that schizophrenia was much more commonly diagnosed in the US than the UK; more recent reports do not indicate this pattern.

A diagnosis of schizophrenia would normally be made following a full psychiatric assessment. This is an extended interview with a trained psychiatrist who will ask about background information and assess a range of symptoms in reaching a view about diagnosis. Two main approaches to diagnosis are the International Classification for Diseases (ICD: most common in the UK and Europe) and the Diagnostic and Statistical Manual (DSM: most common in the US). Both schemes are very strongly related and generate essentially the same primary diagnoses for schizophrenia. Increasingly other clinicians, such as clinical psychologists, are trained in providing clinical diagnoses. Usually the most reliable form of diagnosis is provided when the clinician adheres to a structured clinical interview. This is an interview which carefully asks questions specifically designed to elicit key symptoms and to explore possible diagnoses. The diagnosis is arrived at through the clinical opinion of the person conducting the assessment, on the basis of information obtained from the interview and other sources. A psychiatric diagnosis of this type is therefore not based on objective tests, in contrast to other areas of medicine where blood tests, biopsies or other measures might be used to indicate medical diagnoses.

Who can diagnose schizophrenia?

Many people who are in distress may first approach their general practitioner. Often the initial symptoms of schizophrenia are very disturbing, but it will not always be clear to the individual whether these are caused by physical illness or mental health problems. GPs, or internists, are increasingly aware of the importance of detecting mental health problems in their clinics. A GP may be the first professional to identify that a diagnosis of schizophrenia might be appropriate. However, it is most uncommon for doctors in general practice to have either the training or time to complete a full diagnostic interview. Normally a GP would refer a person they suspected of having schizophrenia on to a local psychiatrist/mental health team for assessment. This will normally consist of a diagnostic interview, as mentioned above, but will usually also draw on information collected from other informants such as caregivers/relatives.

What are the main symptoms of schizophrenia?

The diagnosis of schizophrenia is now quite a reliable one, when made by trained mental health clinicians. However, it is not the case that everyone with schizophrenia is the same. There are numerous sub-categories of schizophrenia and, even within these, individuals will vary. So, before identifying some of the more common symptoms of this diagnosis, it is worth emphasising that this diagnosis is helpful in indicating likely treatment approaches and support, but, the specific patterns of treatment, which will help a specific individual, will have to be a matter for individualised discussion and assessment.

A distinction is often made between positive and negative symptoms of schizophrenia:

Positive symptoms

DELUSIONS

These are beliefs held by an individual in spite of clear evidence to the contrary. Persecutory delusions would generally involve a belief that the person was being followed, investigated, harmed or otherwise 'done down'. In delusions of reference people diagnosed with schizophrenia believe that information from the TV news, records, books or other media is of special significance for them and has been directed at them individually for this purpose. Sometimes delusional beliefs appear to be extensions of thoughts that might be more generally held – such as viewing police as keeping an eye on you, or regarding the government as acting in a harmful way. The distinction here would be the extent to which there was believed to be a specific intent towards you as an individual, in spite of evidence to the contrary. Although this distinction appears clear it is essentially socially defined. Thus, in a particular religious community it might be regarded as relatively common to have beliefs about direct spiritual contact occurring through signs in daily life. However, the same beliefs in general society would possibly be regarded with scepticism. It is therefore important that the clinician making a diagnosis is aware of the extent to which the beliefs an individual holds are consistent with those of his or her peer group. Other examples of delusional beliefs would include beliefs which are called *first rank symptoms* (first labelled as such by the psychiatrist Kurt Schneider). These would include a belief that your mind or body had been taken over by another person or agency; which could include having thoughts extracted or inserted from your mind or having behaviour controlled by others.

Simon was a bright and friendly child, but became increasingly moody and withdrawn as a teenager. He did quite poorly at school and then struggled with his attendance at a local college. He spent more time in his room and began to sleep during the day and to watch television late into the night. Simon later said that during this period he believed that his parents were reading his mind and controlling his behaviour. He thought that his mother was controlling his eating and that when he was having a meal, she was actually eating the food for him. He felt that he could tell when this was happening, from the way his mother looked or from certain words that she said, which he felt had a special significance.

He came to believe that his parents were plotting against him and eventually left home to avoid this. It was only some time later, when Simon had received treatment for his symptoms that he began to be able to analyse these beliefs. He was able to contrast these beliefs with the previously strong relationship that he had had with his parents. Although there continued to be some tensions between Simon and his parents (who were still struggling to understand what had happened), they began to be able to communicate again and work towards rebuilding their relationship.

HALLUCINATIONS

A hallucination is essentially a sensory experience in the absence of an external stimulus. This can occur in any modality (e.g. tastes, sight, touch, smell, hearing) and is not necessarily indicative of schizophrenia. This could include seeing things that are not physically present, feeling as though you are in physical contact with a person or object when there is nothing there, or tasting something without having anything in your mouth. It is not uncommon for hallucinations to occur under extremes of tiredness, following drug or alcohol abuse or in extremes of emotional distress. It is also quite common for hallucinatory experiences to occur as people are falling asleep or waking up. These do not generally have any diagnostic significance for mental health problems.

It is more characteristic of schizophrenia that hallucinations occur in clear consciousness, that is, when the person is fully awake and alert. Furthermore, the key form of hallucinations observed in schizophrenia tends to be auditory. This is the experience of spoken voices, in particular two or more voices in conversation or a single voice commentating on the individual's thoughts and behaviour. The content of these hallucinations can vary from relatively neutral or positive to extremely critical and distressing. Clearly, the experience of hearing hostile disembodied voices commenting on you or the people around you is very distressing and is commonly associated with great confusion and even terror. As it is only the individual who experiences these voices, his or her distress, although clearly evident, may appear incomprehensible to others. This problem may be more difficult if the individual is too distressed or frightened to describe the nature of their experience.

Jemma first became unwell at university. She was very concerned about her coursework and exams. She was also finding that the people she shared a house with were very different from her. As a result, there were arguments in the house and she began to feel increasingly lonely and isolated. One night, lying on her bed, she began to hear two of her flatmates talking about her. Their voices were very clear and she was very upset with what she heard. They were talking about how poorly she was doing in her course ('Jemma is hopeless, she is really dumb'; 'I don't know what she thinks she is doing, she will never pass') and how she was letting her family down ('I'd be embarrassed if I was her mother'; 'I bet her dad just wanted her to get a job; what a waste of money'). Jemma was so upset by this experience that she did not question whether or not the voices were real. She eventually became so distressed that she confided in a friend. Fortunately this friend responded supportively and listened to Jemma's concerns. Eventually she persuaded Jemma to seek help from her doctor. Although there had been conflicts in the house, it later transpired that the voices she had heard could not have been real, as the individuals had not been in the house at the time. Jemma found that medication helped to calm her thoughts and reduce the intensity of these experiences.

THOUGHT DISORDER

This is the presence of breaks or interruptions in trains of thought. This is usually evidenced by disrupted patterns of speech (such as shifting suddenly from one topic to another), apparently irrelevant speech or inclusion of invented or meaningless words. Clearly some disorder in thought is common in all of us. Therefore this needs to reach a significant level, which noticeably interferes with communication, for it to be of relevance as a possible symptom.

Grossly disorganised behaviour would also be included under this broad heading. It includes catatonic symptoms, which are extreme levels of activity (excitement) or inactivity (stupor) unrelated to stimulation provided by the immediate environment. It also includes difficulties with activities of daily living such as dressing, hygiene and sexual behaviour. Again these deviations must be gross, rather than merely evidence of eccentricity.

Jim worked as a painter and decorator at his uncle's painting firm. He enjoyed his work and found that he had a good income and few responsibilities. As a young man he began to go to clubs and to experiment with drugs. However, when he started to feel that other people could read his mind he began to withdraw. He went out less and eventually stopped going to work. He spent long hours alone trying to understand and make sense of his experiences. As his preoccupation with his experiences grew he could talk of little else. His girlfriend, Rachel, found him increasingly difficult to understand. His speech appeared to be disjointed and he referred to experiences that he had had, which he believed everyone else knew about. Although Rachel tried to explain that she did not know about these experiences, Jim did not believe her and often became upset that she was trying to trick him. He would move from topic to topic suddenly, depending on what seemed most important at that moment. Jim did less and less during this period. Where previously he had been proud of his appearance, he began to neglect himself and spend increasing lengths of time shut away in his room. Rachel eventually persuaded him to seek help.

Continued

> Jim found that over time a combination of medication
> and psychological therapy was helpful to him. Gradually
> he managed to focus less on his internal experiences and
> to engage with practical daily tasks.

Negative symptoms

There are a large number of possible negative symptoms. Essentially, negative symptoms are characterised by the absence of either behaviours or experiences that would normally be expected. Again such definitions are to some extent socially defined and the diagnosing clinician must make their judgement with respect to a specific individual's normal social context.

Negative symptoms include:

- Apathy – lacking interest and enthusiasm for activities that had previously been important to them; these might include work activities, hobbies or other interests.
- Reductions in speech – speaking less and being less responsive in conversation, especially where this is in contrast to what would be normal for that person.
- Blunted or incongruous emotional responses – not appearing to react to either happy or sad news, or alternatively appearing to respond with humour to sad news or sadness to positive news.
- Social withdrawal – when an individual cuts him or herself off from friends and family, not wanting to or feeling able to be involved with people.
- Reduced social performance – experiencing problems in conversation, in dealing with day-to-day social situations.

A key problem here is that there are other factors which can cause some similar symptoms to those noted above. Firstly, neuroleptic or anti-psychotic medication is commonly prescribed for the treatment of schizophrenia. Issues associated with this and other medications, are discussed in more detail in chapter 6. However, it is worth noting here, that some of the side effects of anti-psychotic medication can include apathy, sedation and low motivation. Furthermore, depression can also be associated with some or all of the above negative symptoms. It is therefore necessary to rule out the possible contributions from these two sources before attributing these symptoms to schizophrenia.

When Simon was first unwell he would spend increasing amounts of time alone. He began to find it stressful to be with people and felt calmer alone in his bedroom. He found that he wanted to focus on his thoughts and had little energy left for other things. He had less contact with his friends, as he could only really cope with seeing them in his bedroom and avoided going out with them. One factor that his mother found especially distressing during this period was that he appeared not to react when told that his aunt was ill and in hospital. Simon had previously had a very close relationship with his aunt. He had visited her regularly after school as a child, and had also gone on trips with her and her husband when he was a teenager. His mother, who was already upset about her sister's illness, felt at this time that she could no longer 'reach' Simon. Because she was unsure why Simon had responded in this way, she felt frustrated and angry. She was unsure whether this was associated with his illness or whether he no longer cared for someone who had previously seemed to be important to him.

The individual must have experienced at least two key symptoms for a period of a month to meet criteria for a diagnosis of schizophrenia. In addition, there must be evidence of these symptoms causing substantial interference with work, education, family or self-care. There also needs to be evidence of disturbance over a period of at least six months. This may include having fewer symptoms or at a lower intensity than during the specific month-long period. The diagnosis of schizophrenia is not given if symptoms are caused by a medical condition (e.g. epilepsy), substance abuse, or mood disorders such as bipolar disorder.

Sub-types of schizophrenia

There are, according to DSM-IV, the most recent version of the US diagnostic approach, four sub-types of schizophrenia. Other classification systems differ slightly. Essentially these sub-types are intended to serve as summaries of the main symptoms experienced by individuals in each sub-type. Thus in *Paranoid Schizophrenia* the individual is characterised as mainly experiencing delusions and/or hallucinations. However, disorganised speech and behaviour and blunted or incongruous emotional responses would not usually be prominent. In *Disorganised Schizophrenia*, as the term implies, disorganised speech/thought, disorganised behaviour and flat or inappropriate affect (failure to show normal emotional responses) would be the main features. In *Catatonic Schizophrenia*, the key features include motor immobility (lack of normal range of movements), excessive motor activity (moving more frequently and more vigorously than normal), extreme negativism or mutism (lack of speech), posturing or stereotyped movements, echolalia/echopraxia (repetition of the words or actions of others). The term *Undifferentiated Schizophrenia* is used when the symptoms experienced by the individual do not specifically fit with any of the above categories.

The European system (most recent version ICD-10) has the six main categories. *Paranoid schizophrenia* is characterised by delusions, usually accompanied by auditory hallucinations and perceptual disturbances. In *Hebephrenic schizophrenia* mood changes are prominent but delusions and hallucinations are less evident. The mood can seem shallow and inappropriate. Thoughts and speech can be disorganised. There is a tendency to avoid social situations. In *Catatonic schizophrenia* psychomotor disturbances are central. The individual may alternate between extremes of over- and under-activity. Particular physical attitudes and postures may be maintained for long periods. Episodes of extreme excitement may be a feature of the condition. This is now rarely seen in the developed world. The term *Undifferentiated schizophrenia* is used when none of the above categories are appropriate but the individual still meets basic criteria for schizophrenia. *Residual schizophrenia* is a chronic category given to individuals with a history of clear psychotic symptoms, but whose current presentation is of mainly negative symptoms. *Simple schizophrenia* is uncommon. It is characterised by progressive development of oddities of conduct, inability to meet the demands of society and decline in total performance. The negative features of residual schizophrenia appear, without the history of overt psychotic symptoms. Additionally ICD-10 allows for a diagnosis of *post-schizophrenic depression* which is a depressive disorder following on within twelve months of a schizophrenic illness and when some schizophrenic symptoms are still present.

Other related diagnoses

With DSM-IV, there are also a number of related, but distinct, diagnoses for people with symptoms similar to those experienced in schizophrenia. *Schizophreniform disorder* is a diagnosis given when the symptoms and disturbance are present for a month, as opposed to the six months in the case of schizophrenia. Here the additional impairment of social and occupational functioning is not required. A diagnosis of *Schizoaffective disorder* is given when the symptoms of schizophrenia are only present during an episode of major depression, mania or mixed (combined manic and depressed) mood. *Delusional Disorder* is diagnosed when the person is experiencing one or more delusional beliefs which are non-bizarre (such as delusional jealousy). This means that these are not *first rank* symptoms (as described on pp. 20–28).

With *Brief psychotic disorder* there is a duration of one day to a month, with full return to normal functioning after this. At least one of the symptoms of delusions, hallucinations, disorganised speech, grossly disorganised or catatonic behaviour must be noted during this period.

> Sam started to have mood changes soon after she married. She initially had a good relationship with her husband, but this then began to deteriorate. He began to stay out late and had other relationships. At the same time Sam's parents became ill and they were increasingly dependent on her. She found that her mood would be very low for periods of several days and would then sometimes swing up so that she felt very active and positive. When her mood was depressed Sam became aware of voices that she did not recognise criticising her as a wife and daughter. The voices were very hostile and told her that when she found it difficult to motivate herself she was just being lazy. Although these experiences were very distressing, when her mood lifted the voices did not persist. Sam eventually sought help both for her mood problems and for the voices which distressed her when her mood was low. Sam received a diagnosis of schizoaffective disorder.

Some people may well have emotional problems which lead them to seek help from mental health professionals. If there are persistent features of the person's behaviour that indicate experiences within the broad spectrum of schizophrenia-like symptoms, but which are not explained by any of the above, then one of the following diagnoses may be applied.

1. *Paranoid personality disorder* is indicated by a pervasive distrust and suspiciousness of others. It is usually indicated by

repeatedly interpreting the motives behind the behaviour of others as malevolent (seeking to do harm to you) on the basis of little or no real evidence.

2. *Schizoid personality disorder* is a diagnosis which applies to people who have a pervasive pattern of detachment from social relationships and restricted emotional range from early adulthood. This means that people will usually have a very limited range of friends and other contacts and may well find social situations difficult to deal with. In terms of interaction with other people, there will be an observable tendency to appear aloof or distanced, so that when emotionally important events occur these will not appear to impact on the person.

3. *Schizotypal personality disorder* is associated with a pervasive pattern of social and interpersonal problems marked by acute discomfort with close relationships, unusual beliefs and experiences, and eccentricities of behaviour.

Emotional distress

We have discussed the key symptoms that are identified by mental health professionals when schizophrenia is being diagnosed. However, the diagnostic systems used to make this diagnosis do not emphasise the emotional distress that is commonly experienced by people with these symptoms. When discussing the course of their illness the key features that many people will highlight are feelings of trauma, terror, loneliness, fear, sadness, emptiness and depression. These are important to the person and also key to managing the illness itself. As indicated in chapter 7, a psychological approach to schizophrenia is about living with and managing this set of experiences.

Often the experience of hallucinations is not, of itself, the primary problem that people have. More often it is trying to make sense of the significance of this experience, and also of other people's interpretations of it, that is crucial. Thus, many people may be able to cope well with life, even if they continue to experience regular schizophrenic symptoms, as long as they are able to interpret these experiences in ways which do not cause them significant fear, distress or disruption.

In addition, people's thoughts and feelings about their experiences before and during their illness are important. This will include the reactions of family and friends, the response of the criminal justice system and the approaches taken by mental health services. Indeed there is recent evidence from studies in the UK and the US that many people with psychosis experience symptoms akin to *Post Traumatic Stress Disorder* (PTSD). PTSD is a disorder associated with the experience of an intensely frightening event in which the individual experiences a substantial threat to themselves or those close to them. As indicated above, the beliefs and experiences associated with the onset of schizophrenia can in themselves be terrifying and constitute a very severe perceived threat to the individual. Symptoms of PTSD itself can include having events run over and over in the person's mind, being unable to concentrate or relax, being very distractable, and being very easily startled by sudden sounds. In addition, individuals may seek to avoid people, as well as objects and situations associated with their trauma. An understanding of these symptoms can therefore be important in understanding the particular pattern of difficulties with which an individual with a diagnosis of schizophrenia might present.

It is also known that depression is common among people with schizophrenia and is often associated with insight into the nature of schizophrenia. Thus, people who agree with their doctors about their diagnosis, appear sometimes to be more depressed than those who do not. There have been various explanations for this, but the most likely seems to be that if people only see themselves as having a biological illness over which they have little control, depression is predictable. However, as is clear from this book and other work, there is much that an individual can do to influence the course of their own illness, even if they might also find that medication has an important role in maintaining their mental health.

It should therefore be clear that there are a wide range of emotional factors in addition to the specific diagnosis of schizophrenia. It is therefore critical that there is an understanding of the emotional consequences of schizophrenia, so that appropriate help and support can be focused on the key needs of the individual, not solely on symptoms taken into consideration in diagnosis.

A caveat to diagnostic information

As indicated in chapter 1, we are well aware that many people who have a diagnosis of schizophrenia may well not agree with this. This can equally apply to people placed in some of the other diagnostic categories listed above. We see the role of this book as being to summarise available information in an accessible format, rather than to persuade individuals concerning the validity of particular diagnostic criteria. Therefore this chapter seeks to inform service users and caregivers about the current terms used by mental health services and hence to demystify them. We are aware that such terms can be important for communication between professionals and for research, but also that they have limitations. We would reiterate that if you have experiences that cause you distress, even if you feel the overall diagnostic label is unhelpful, you may well find the information contained here of benefit.

Points covered in this chapter

➡ There is no objective test for schizophrenia: diagnosis is based on clinical interview and associated information. There are two main diagnostic schemes used in the UK and the US, both of which are now reliable.

➡ Schizophrenia is normally diagnosed by a psychiatrist or other mental health professional. The most reliable diagnoses are made through structured clinical interviews.

➡ There are a number of characteristic symptoms of schizophrenia, but patterns of symptoms will vary from person to person.

➡ Positive symptoms of schizophrenia include delusional beliefs, hallucinations and thought disorder. The clinician needs to ensure that these symptoms are assessed with reference to the person's social norms, as the criteria for 'normal beliefs' will depend on cultural and religious factors, among others.

➡ Negative symptoms of schizophrenia include apathy, reductions in speech, blunted emotional responses, and social difficulties. These symptoms again should be assessed with regard to the person's normal social context. Mood difficulties and medication side effects can also be associated with negative symptoms.

➡ There are a number of diagnoses related to schizophrenia in which symptoms are less pervasive or severe. These include schizophreniform disorder, schizoaffective disorder, delusional disorder and brief psychotic disorder.

➡ Irrespective of particular symptoms, people's main priorities are often dealing with the emotional consequences of their mental health problems and making sense of their experiences and other people's reactions to these.

➡ Emotional distress can be severe and some people with schizophrenia experience symptoms consistent with post traumatic stress disorder.

➡ This chapter aims to summarise diagnostic information accessibly, so that the reader can reach their own conclusion about how they feel any psychiatric label they have received may or may not apply to them.

4

Myths about schizophrenia

It is interesting to note that some diseases inspire a great deal of fear and worry, while often, others are ignored by the general public. Diseases of the liver and kidneys are very serious and potentially fatal, yet few people worry about them. Cancer and AIDS are serious diseases, but people often fear them and worry about them to a much greater extent than other equally serious illnesses such as heart disease. In the field of mental health, bipolar disorder is just as common as schizophrenia, but members of the public are much less likely to have heard of it. Schizophrenia is a word that is often used in a variety of contexts, a word that many people are likely to have heard. This does not mean, however, that people are well informed; in fact, research evidence suggests that most laypeople know very little about any aspect of mental illness. Instead, many people, including some sufferers, believe a number of myths about schizophrenia, myths that can frighten them and cause them to avoid and distrust those who suffer from the illness.

Myth: Schizophrenia means having a 'split personality'

The term 'schizophrenia' was originally coined by Bleuler, a Swiss psychiatrist who practised around the turn of the last century, who used it to describe a group of patients whom he observed in the asylum where he worked. The term 'schizophrenia' means 'split mind' in Greek: Bleuler used it to describe what he believed were 'splits' in the thoughts, actions and feelings of patients. For example, a patient might talk about something very distressing in a cheerful way, and Bleuler considered this as a split between thoughts and feelings. Bleuler thought that this splitting was a defining characteristic of the illness, but no modern psychiatrist or psychologist would agree with this. Nevertheless, Bleuler's work was influential, and his term came into general use.

Unfortunately, the term schizophrenic came to be confused in the minds of many people with the 'split personality', a type of Jekyll and Hyde person often seen in movies or featured in thrillers but very rare in real life. This person is sometimes pictured in fictional works as kind and sweet on the outside but hiding a violent, dangerous personality that emerges without warning. Popular works of psychology also refer to a form of psychiatric illness called 'multiple personality disorder', in which one person will manifest a number of different personalities, which may each have different names and behave in different ways. This is a relatively rare phenomenon, much more common in literature than in real life, and it has nothing to do with schizophrenia. In addition, the term schizophrenic is also used in general language to mean being 'of two minds'. A commentator might say, for example, 'The Government is schizophrenic on this issue: they say they want to help business, yet they raise business taxes.' This is a perfectly valid use of the word, but of course has nothing to do with schizophrenia as a clinical diagnosis.

This myth is unhelpful because it leads people to think that those with schizophrenia are uniquely unpredictable and dangerous. Of course, sufferers may show shifting moods, especially if they are experiencing disturbing symptoms. Someone being insulted and harassed by voices or persecutory beliefs might well lash out in anger, but this is true of almost anyone; even the most mild-mannered person can become angry given the right circumstances. The friends and family of sufferers, once they have come to understand their symptoms, can usually form a very good idea of how they are likely to behave in different circumstances.

Myth: All schizophrenics are violent and dangerous

This is a very common myth, and obviously a very frightening one. Like the previous one, it grows out of an image of the mentally ill as completely unpredictable and likely to do extreme things for no reason. There have been a few incidents in which mental illness sufferers have killed or injured strangers in unprovoked attacks, and the amount of publicity that these events have received in the media has made them seem much more common than they are. In fact, people diagnosed with schizophrenia and other serious mental illness are much more likely to harm themselves than to harm others, and much more likely to be the victims of crime than the perpetrators.

Much of the worry about violence by the mentally ill has centred around the policy of 'care in the community' or 'de-institutionalisation'. Many large asylums have been closed, and many mentally ill people are living in the community, often very successfully. It is true that patients in the community can be unwell, and can sometimes have to return to hospital. However, statistics show that the closure of the asylums and the care in the community policy have not led to any increase in crimes of violence by mentally ill people. Statistics also show that crimes of violence, including murder, assault, wounding and rape, are generally committed by men rather than women, by the young rather than the old and, often, by those who have been drinking alcohol. However, no one has dreamed of suggesting that all young men who drink alcohol are dangerous and should be controlled or locked up.

When Jemma was first ill she was afraid that the fact that she was hearing voices would make people think she was 'a psycho' and that she might become violent for no reason. Fortunately, her friends were able to reassure her about his, stating that they always knew her to be a kind person who 'wouldn't hurt a fly'. During a heated argument with his parents Simon once smashed a vase that belonged to his mother; this upset her at the time but has now been long forgotten, and it is the only time that Simon has ever done anything 'violent'.

Myth: People with serious mental illness are completely disabled

I remember hearing a joke told when I was young; it concerned a man who has a flat tyre in front of a 'lunatic asylum'. Having removed the wheel he inadvertently loses the nuts that are used to attach it down a drain. He is completely at a loss, until one of the inmates, who has been watching from the other side of a fence, suggests to him that he take one nut from each of the other three wheels and use them to attach the spare tyre until he can drive to a garage. The man is very pleased by this helpful suggestion, but a bit puzzled by the fact that a 'crazy person' has been able to think of it. When he comments on this, the inmate replies, 'Well, I may be crazy, but I'm not stupid.'

Like most jokes, this joke derives whatever humour it has from cultural attitudes and values. It clearly betrays two assumptions about mental illness. First, it implies that those with schizophrenia and other serious illnesses need to be isolated and kept away from others, perhaps because they are dangerous and incapable of normal human interaction. Second, the motorist clearly believes that anyone who is 'crazy' is incapable of normal, rational thought, and certainly of thought that involves intelligence and creativity. In fact, however, the joke conveys a correct message: those with mental illness are no more or less intelligent than anyone else.

In fact, the motorist is not alone in believing that those with mental illness are 'irrational' and incapable of self-care. Few laypeople would probably state this as a fact, but it is an assumption that can colour the way people think. In fact, those with mental illnesses, including schizophrenia, bipolar disorder and even depression, are often thought to be less capable than others of managing their lives. Such attitudes, often subconsciously held, can influence the way members of the public deal with people with many types of problems and disabilities. This feeling was captured by a radio programme for disabled people that used to be broadcast on the BBC. The programme was called, 'Does he take sugar?' It seems to be the experience of people with many types of disabilities that others assume they are not capable of making the simplest decisions.

Anyone who has dealt with people with schizophrenia will know that they are no more or less intelligent than anyone else. As explained above, certain patients, when acutely unwell, may find it difficult to think clearly, but this symptom usually disappears or improves to a very great extent with treatment. In most cases, patients will usually show odd patterns of thinking when discussing their unusual beliefs and experiences, such as delusions and hallucinations. Interestingly, some patients can show a high degree of creative thinking and skill in argument when defending their unusual or different views of the world. And often patients can show unusual intelligence and creative ability in areas unconnected to their illnesses.

A historical example illustrating this fact is the story of William Chester Minor, described in the book *The Surgeon of Crowthorne* by Simon Winchester. Minor, an American surgeon living in London during Victorian times, murdered a passer-by because he believed that the man was part of a group of people who were persecuting him and forcing him to commit perverted sexual acts. He was confined for many years in Broadmoor Special Hospital, but, being a man with considerable private means and a great lover of books, he filled his quarters with numerous old and rare books that he had collected. At this time the *Oxford English Dictionary* was being compiled, and the editor relied on amateur scholars to provide examples of the uses of particular words in books written in various historical periods. Minor became one of the key amateur contributors to the *Dictionary,* supplying literally thousands of examples from a range of interesting and obscure books. James Murray, the editor, visited Minor, and was struck by his considerable learning. Unfortunately, at the same time that he was performing this important scholarly work, Minor remained convinced that numerous people were invading his rooms in the night and tormenting him in unspeakable ways, a belief that continued to trouble him throughout his life. Of course, at the time that Minor was living little was known about the causes of mental illness and no effective treatments were available.

Myth: Having schizophrenia means that you can never do anything with your life

This point follows on from the previous one. If people believe that a mental illness diagnosis means that you are completely incapable, then it would be logical to also believe that sufferers would be completely disabled and unable to do anything with their lives. As we have tried to make clear, the outcome following a diagnosis of schizophrenia is very variable: many sufferers either recover completely or suffer only with residual symptoms that can be controlled through medication and psychological techniques. Sufferers go on to hold good jobs, marry, have children, and live 'normal' lives. In cases where symptoms are more severe and harder to control, doing these things may be more difficult, although still possible in many cases. As we hope to make clear, even those with the most severe and disabling symptoms can still do much to improve the quality of their lives and succeed in a variety of areas.

When Jemma was first told that she had a psychotic illness, she assumed that this meant that she would face a lifetime of disability. Fortunately she had supportive friends who believed in her. They knew her to be an intelligent and able person and reassured her that her intelligence and ability would allow her to overcome her illness. She is now working full time and has only had to miss work for a few short periods when her voices have become too intrusive. One friend of hers suffers with chronic asthma and has had to have periods off work following severe asthma attacks. Jemma finds it useful to talk to her friend, and they compare notes about the difficulties of living with their respective illnesses.

Myth: Mental hospitals are 'bedlams'

The term 'bedlam', referring to a scene of frenzied, senseless activity, comes from the Bethlem Hospital, the first mental hospital in Britain. It reflects the fact that large numbers of people, many of whom acted in bizarre ways, were confined for long periods of time in the Bethlem and places like it. There was a time, perhaps lasting until the middle of the twentieth century, when there was little effective treatment for serious mental illness. Such hospitals would also have visits from members of the public who regarded people with mental illness as objects of curiosity rather than individuals requiring help and support to get on with their lives.

At that time the only medication available to treat mental patients was sedative medication that made them sleep but did not relieve their symptoms, and the majority of mental hospitals were places of confinement rather than treatment. In those days mental hospitals were often very large, with thousands of beds, and patients might spend years or even decades on the back wards, receiving very little care. Various ineffective treatments were used, for example electroconvulsive therapy, or 'shock therapy'; this treatment can have beneficial effects in some cases of depression but is not really appropriate for other kinds of mental illness. In the nineteenth century other inhumane forms of treatment and control, such as for example the straitjacket, were also used. All this created an image of mental health treatment that was both frightening and barbaric.

Unfortunately, images like these still influence the way many people think about mental health treatment today. In fact, there has been a complete revolution in all areas of treatment for mental and psychological problems. As we hope to show throughout this book, there are now a variety of effective treatments for major mental illnesses. Similarly, the old days of the huge asylum where patients spent years in hospital are now past; modern mental health treatment can be expensive, and hospitals are under pressure to discharge patients and to care for them, as much as possible, in their own homes. Today both practical and clinical considerations mean that people are only kept in hospital for as long as is absolutely necessary. The old images of mental health treatment are not useful guides as to what happens today.

Myth: Schizophrenia represents a form of creative imagination or 'inner journey'

Ordinary people generally hold negative views about schizophrenia, but there are exceptions. In the 1960s we recall that some people used to make great claims for the power of hallucinogenic drugs to change people's lives in a positive way. There were some people, usually those who had never had any dealings with people with serious mental illness, who believed that schizophrenia represented a form of superior creative insight into the nature of reality, and that the experience of mental illness was comparable to that induced by using drugs. It is sometimes believed that those with mental illness have fallen ill because of their greater sensitivity to the world, or even that the odd beliefs of those with mental illness are in reality a form of heightened awareness. Sometimes highly creative people are thought to be closer to 'madness' than the rest of us, and it is certainly true that some artists, from the French poets Baudelaire and Rimbaud to the novelist Ken Kesey, have taken various drugs in an attempt to become more 'creative'.

 A good example of this viewpoint is contained in Kesey's novel *One Flew Over the Cuckoo's Nest*. The rebellious hero McMurphy allows himself to be confined in an asylum to escape criminal charges, but ultimately he leads a rebellion by the other inmates against the oppressive rule of the Big Nurse. The novel is seen through the eyes of the mentally ill Indian, Chief Broom, and Chief Broom's psychotic ideas are often metaphors for what is happening among the other patients and staff. Kesey's novel is a brilliant piece of writing and can be seen as describing the struggle of the human spirit against oppression, but

Continued

> it is a very poor guide to current psychiatric practice, in the same way that *Moby Dick* can be considered both a masterpiece of world literature and a very poor source of information about current commercial fishing practices.

There have certainly been examples of creative writers, artists and musicians who have suffered from schizophrenia and other forms of serious mental illness. Similarly, the Nobel Prize-winning mathematician John Nash suffered from schizophrenia, as shown in the book *A Beautiful Mind* by Sylvia Nasar, made into a film starring Russell Crowe. Great artists and other creative thinkers make use of all their experiences in their work, but it is our view that, in general, highly creative sufferers are highly creative people anyway, and their illnesses are not the cause of their abilities. People who suffer from schizophrenia, as with most illnesses, will show the full range of human strengths, weaknesses, talents and abilities. Effective help for sufferers should therefore make them more creative and effective people.

 Since his hospitalisation Jim has been prone, at times, to become excited about some particular idea that he reads about or hears about on television. He is particularly interested in ideas about spirituality and paranormal mental powers. At times Jim feels that he has some special insight into the nature of reality or the meaning and purpose of human existence. At the same time, he has learnt that he can't really communicate or explain these ideas to others. He has found that it helps to think of himself as a 'spiritual person', one who might see a meaning or significance in things that other people can't see. Jim's girlfriend, Rachel, tends to be a much more sceptical person. Through trial and error they have now

Continued

> learnt to get along and avoid arguing over these differences. Jim can now accept that Rachel is unlikely to share his particular insights, while she understands that they have great significance for him.

Myth: It's all in the genes so there's nothing you can do

There is considerable evidence that genetic factors can play a role in the development of schizophrenia. In a similar way, the action of anti-psychotic drugs suggests that various chemicals in the brain can play a role in producing the symptoms of psychosis. It is to be hoped that research in these areas will throw more light on the causes of psychotic illnesses and lead to more effective treatments. However, the fact that some of the causes of schizophrenic symptoms may lie 'in the brain' or 'in the genes' can be interpreted by sufferers and their families as meaning, 'Nothing can be done', or 'Medication is the only treatment'. As we hope this book will make clear, there are a variety of things that sufferers and their families can do to improve their situations. Research evidence continues to accumulate that suggests that a variety of interventions, such as: 1) reducing family stress; 2) improving the financial and occupational situation; 3) promoting fulfilling activities of all sorts; and 4) using the various forms of therapy discussed in this book, can all improve the quality of life of people with schizophrenia.

The course of a schizophrenic illness can be very varied; many sufferers have been acutely unwell but later recovered fully and never fallen ill again. Even those with very severe and chronic illness can improve over the course of time. Further, as already noted, factors like genetic disposition do not doom a person to illness; even among identical twins, who share the same genetic makeup, a psychotic illness in one twin does not mean that the other is doomed to fall ill also. The current state of knowledge really does not allow us to predict the course of schizophrenic illness, but we can predict that an attitude of hopelessness and negativity is unlikely to promote positive changes and improved functioning. For this reason, we try throughout this book to offer a message of hope and to suggest ways that the situations of sufferers can be improved.

Myth: It's all the parents' fault

This idea is fortunately much less common than it used to be. It goes back to Sigmund Freud and his followers, who believed that schizophrenic illnesses were due to poor parenting, especially by the mother, which resulted in the child being unable to deal with reality. Some later thinkers have attributed schizophrenia to poor patterns of communication in the family, which lead to confusion on the part of the child. As will be explained in chapter 10, the behaviour of family members can have an influence on the course of illness. However, there is no evidence whatsoever to support the idea that poor parenting is the cause of schizophrenia. Rather than blaming themselves, family members can learn how to help their loved one to manage better, an idea to which we will return.

Myth: They're not trying/Myth: It's hopeless; they can never get better

Ignorant people sometimes believe that those with mental illness ought to be able to 'pull themselves together'. After all, the reasoning goes, the problem is in the mind, and people can control their own minds, so sufferers ought to be able to resolve their problems. On the other hand, other equally ignorant people believe that 'crazy' people are hopeless cases, not like the rest of us, whose condition can never improve. Both these myths are equally unhelpful, the first because it encourages people to judge and condemn the mentally ill, the second because it suggests that nothing can be done. We hope that this book will suggest a third approach. Those with serious mental illness cannot simply 'pull themselves together', but there are many things they can do, with the help of their families and various professionals, to better their situation. What they need from others is understanding, encouragement and support in positive activities; what they need from themselves is patience and willingness to seek for help and solutions to their problems. As noted throughout this chapter, the most important message is the message of hope.

When Jim first became ill, he was very reluctant to seek help, or even to tell others about his experiences. As he finally said to his girlfriend, he believed that if he told anyone what was happening, they would think that he was 'mental'. This was very frightening to Jim. He knew very little about mental illness, but he had heard his parents talk about his great uncle, who had fought in the First World War and subsequently spent many years in an asylum. His great uncle was little talked about, as his problems were a source of shame and embarrassment to the family, but he supposedly behaved very oddly and accused members of the family of trying to steal his money, of which he claimed to have a great deal, although there was no evidence that this was the case. Jim's image of a mentally ill person was of someone like his uncle, who was confined in an asylum, behaved oddly and could not be helped. Fortunately, Jim now realises that, had his uncle been alive today, he would probably not have had to spend his life in hospital. He is also able to be much more matter of fact about his own mental health problems, and to see these problems as something that he can manage if he is receiving the right kind of help.

Points covered in this chapter

➡ Many popular myths hinder proper understanding of terms like schizophrenia. It is the intention of this book to provide information that will counter these myths.

➡ Schizophrenia does not refer to a 'split personality'.

➡ The image of people with schizophrenia as violent and dangerous is highly exaggerated.

➡ The term 'schizophrenia' does not imply helplessness or incapacity.

➡ Those diagnosed with schizophrenia show the same range of talents and abilities as anyone else.

➡ Continued advances in our knowledge of the causes and treatment of mental illness are reflected in a much improved quality of care.

➡ Current evidence suggests that genetic factors may be important in causing the symptoms of schizophrenia, but this should not be taken to mean that nothing can be done.

➡ There is no evidence that poor parenting is a cause of schizophrenia. There is however evidence that family relationships can have an important impact on the course of schizophrenia.

➡ A diagnosis of schizophrenia does not rule out improvement and positive change.

5

Treatments for schizophrenia – professional help

Dealing with professionals

Mental health professionals have often had a bad press. In films and books they are often portrayed either as rather comical psychoanalysts, who use odd words and are more neurotic than their patients, or as sinister control freaks, whose goal is to lock people up in mental hospitals and give them large amounts of unnecessary medication. Being mental health professionals ourselves, our view is different: we see our fellow professionals as a varied group of people, generally dedicated to their work, but with varying talents and abilities. Certainly working with people who suffer from mental health problems is a tricky job, and no professional can claim to have always made the right decision or to have treated every patient with the optimal amount of care and courtesy. In spite of this, we feel that the system of mental health care in most Western countries can provide important help to many people suffering from a variety of problems. Here we offer a brief guide to the various professional groups and what sorts of help they might offer.

If you have had bad experiences with the mental health system in the past, we urge you not to let these experiences put you off taking advantage of the help that you might be offered. If you feel that your care has been seriously mishandled, you may well wish to complain to some official body. This might seem like a lot of trouble, but it might be a more helpful thing to do than to simply avoid professionals and thus not receive any treatment or help. If possible, the best alternative is to look for a worker or set of workers that you can relate to, someone whom you feel treats you with respect. Training in medicine and related disciplines is putting increased emphasis on developing a good relationship with consumers of mental health services. We hope that you will persist and believe that, with persistence, most people can find a professional with whom they can work.

Care settings

Mental health care can be delivered in a variety of settings. Traditionally, people with serious mental illness were treated in hospitals. Before the invention of current drug treatments, mental hospitals were often extremely large, with, at times, thousands of beds. Because there was no effective treatment, patients might spend years, or even a lifetime, in such settings. However, this sort of treatment is very much a thing of the past. The old hospitals have been closed and their sites have often been redeveloped into housing or business premises. Modern hospitals are much smaller, and the length of time that patients spend in them is correspondingly much less. Patients will only stay in hospital when they are acutely unwell, and otherwise they will often be treated in the community, as outpatients.

Such outpatient treatment may also take place in hospital clinics, but this is no longer universally the case. Increasingly care is being delivered in settings in the community, such as Community Mental Health Teams in the UK or Health

Maintenance Organisations and Community Mental Health Clinics in the US. In both hospital and community settings patients will have access to a varied group of professionals, often referred to as a Multi-Disciplinary Team (MDT). Often members of such teams will see patients in their own homes or in other settings away from hospital sites.

In this chapter we will talk about the various members of an MDT and their roles. Finally, for those with private resources or private health insurance, the services of various professionals can also be obtained privately. In that case, professionals will often be based in private clinics or consulting offices.

Psychiatrists

If people are asked to name the professional who deals with people with mental illness, they will usually say, 'A psychiatrist'. This is true, but many people don't have much of an idea of who psychiatrists are or what they do. The short answer is that they are qualified medical doctors who have had specialist training in the care of people with mental and emotional problems. Like all doctors, they will have been through medical school and received general training in medicine and surgery. Any doctor who specialises will then work for several more years in their chosen speciality, first working in a junior role, supervised by more senior colleagues, and then rising up to more senior positions and eventually reaching a position of independent authority. Such doctors are called Consultants in the UK (the term we generally use) and Attending Physicians (Attendings for short) in the US. In general, the ultimate responsibility for patient care rests with Consultants, but more junior doctors do much of the day-to-day clinical work. This is true in medical specialties such as dermatology or oncology, and it is also true in psychiatry. Patients who attend the same hospital or clinic for a number of years often complain that their doctor keeps changing; this is because the doctor is very often a junior doctor, and junior doctors change jobs periodically so as to learn about all aspects of their chosen specialism. This can be irritating for the patient, but it does ensure that when doctors do rise to the highest level, they have had a wide variety of training and experience. They should also be in a good position to oversee the work of more junior medical staff.

Most psychiatrists would probably describe their job as the diagnosis and treatment of mental disorder. Of these, the practice of diagnosis is not unique to psychiatrists, since most mental health professionals will be able to apply diagnostic labels. As in most areas of medicine, the first line of psychiatric treatment is usually medication. At present, only doctors can prescribe medications, and this is probably appropriate, as their training in all aspects of medical care is generally more extensive than that of any other professional group. However, this is an issue that has been the subject of debate, with some pilot schemes giving limited prescribing rights to other health professionals following additional training. A psychiatrist will generally prescribe a particular medication and then offer follow-up appointments to monitor its effects and adjust the dosage. Chapter 6 offers a discussion of the various types of medication often prescribed for schizophrenia and other psychotic illnesses. At the same time, doctors are supposed to be familiar with all aspects of treatment, including psychological and social approaches and health management advice, and ideally they should be able to enlist the help and advice of other professionals who are experts in these areas. Doctors are increasingly receiving specialist training in other aspects of treatment, a trend that we would feel to be beneficial, especially since a Consultant Psychiatrist is ideally supposed to oversee all aspects of a patient's care, both during hospital admissions and while patients are living in the community.

Being detained in hospital

There is one important difference between psychiatrists and other medical specialists: psychiatrists are the only doctors who have the legal right to force patients to accept treatment and to keep them in hospital if they refuse treatment. In our own professional work we have seen this happen on many occasions, and we have mixed feelings about it. On the one hand, we know that for many patients the experience of being forced to stay in hospital against their will can be very distressing. There are a number of reasons for this. First, there is the simple fact that you are suddenly not in control of your own life. Doctors and nurses can prevent you from leaving even to take a walk around the block, and they may force you to take medication against your will or attend meetings when you are not interested. In addition, most psychiatric wards are not pleasant places. They are often full of people in various states of distress or anger, and they may also offer very little in the way of entertainment or distraction. For all these reasons, it is very natural for people to feel negative about what has happened to them. On the other hand, we have seen cases in which involuntary hospitalisation has been, quite literally, life-saving.

 When Jim first became ill, Rachel, his girlfriend, persuaded him to attend an appointment with a local mental health team. At this point, Jim was finding it very difficult to look after himself, including basic tasks such as washing and eating, he was socially isolated, and at times he was so distressed that he felt suicidal. He was persuaded to come into hospital as a voluntary patient, but he then decided to leave. The medical and nursing staff were so worried about him that they prevented

Continued

> him from leaving and ordered his involuntary detention.
> Jim was at first very angry about this and complained
> bitterly, but after a few weeks he began to feel better,
> and even agreed to stay for an extra week as a volun-
> tary patient when he was no longer detained. Jim still
> believes that his detention was unnecessary and that he
> would have been all right at home rather than in hos-
> pital. Rachel is not so sure; she believes that Jim's life
> might have been in danger if he had been at home rather
> than in hospital.

When thinking about the rights and wrongs of involuntary detention, it is worth bearing in mind that the right to detain people is
carefully controlled by law. Mental health laws in most English-
speaking countries are broadly similar. They generally require
the agreement of a number of professionals before someone can
be detained. Further, these professionals have to agree on three
general points. First, to be detained a person has to be diagnosed
as suffering from a mental illness, second, the person has to represent a danger, either to themselves or someone else, and third,
the person has to be refusing treatment. Detention is for a fixed
period of time, usually somewhere between one and six months,
and the patient's condition has to be reviewed regularly to make
sure that there is still a need for further detention. There is generally a legal obligation on medical and nursing staff to make
sure that the detained patient is well aware of his or her rights.
Finally, there are legal safeguards designed to prevent unnecessary detentions. For example, in the United Kingdom there is
a Mental Health Act Commission (the contact information is
contained in Appendix 1) that regularly reviews the legal status of patients in hospital. Detained patients can appeal to the
Commission and can attend hearings to argue their cases, aided
by lawyers paid for by the commission. Similar systems exist
in the US, though these usually differ from state to state. We

have seen patients released prior to such hearings taking place because the medical team feels that the hearing will find in their favour. We believe that the existence of such appeal processes can be very helpful in giving detained patients a sense of dignity and self-worth; even if an appeal is not successful, patients will often say that they have gained a valuable sense that they had been listened to and their views respected.

In spite of these various safeguards, enforced treatment is often very unpleasant and can cause a great deal of resentment on the part of the patient. If this has happened to you, it can prove a real barrier to seeking help in the future. We have no easy answer to this point, except to say that it is probably better, if you can, to overlook unpleasant past events if they are proving to be a barrier to getting help you need. Furthermore, our experience suggests that if you can take an active role in your own care and also ask for help, if you require it, at an early stage, it substantially reduces the likelihood of situations deteriorating to the point that enforced treatment is required. However, if you do feel that you have been a victim of injustice, there are ways of complaining that we will deal with later in this book.

When Simon was first ill he spent several weeks in a London hospital. This experience was very distressing for him, and he had a number of bad memories associated with it. In particular, he did not like the conditions and food on the ward where he was detained, and he felt that one of his doctors was very abrupt and patronising. He considered appealing against his detention but was discharged before the appeal hearing could be scheduled. Many years later he wrote a letter of complaint to the hospital describing his experiences and demanding an

Continued

apology. He did in fact receive a letter of apology and he was also asked if he wished to make a formal complaint about the particular doctor. In the end he decided not to do this, but he did feel better after writing the letter and receiving an apology. He was also pleased that he had begun the appeal process, feeling that he had done something active to stand up for his own rights.

Clinical psychologists

As mentioned in the last section and discussed in more detail in chapter 6, psychiatric medications constitute one of the most common forms of treatment for schizophrenia, and also for many other forms of mental illness. However, a complementary approach focusing on psychological treatment has become better known in recent years. This is especially true in the United Kingdom, where a government body, the National Institute for Clinical Excellence, has recommended that psychological treatment be available to all patients with serious mental illness. We discuss psychological treatments in more detail in chapter 6, but here we offer some brief comments on the professionals who deliver psychological therapies.

One professional group, Clinical Psychologists, devotes itself primarily to the delivery of various forms of psychological assessment and treatment. Clinical Psychologists have generally studied the academic discipline of Psychology as undergraduates and gone on to earn a further postgraduate degree that allows them to deliver psychological therapies. The majority of Clinical Psychologists in most countries now have doctoral level qualifications, although of course they are not medical doctors and cannot prescribe drugs. (In some countries it has been suggested that they might be licensed to prescribe certain medications, but this has yet to be implemented.) Clinical Psychologists then generally go on to develop advanced expertise in some particular area of specialisation, and many of them receive training in Cognitive Behavioural Therapy (CBT). They may also have other jobs, such as teaching or doing research. A related field is that of Counselling Psychology; Counselling Psychologists undergo a training similar to that of Clinical Psychologists and often utilise the same sorts of therapeutic techniques.

In addition to Psychologists, members of many other professions can choose to develop expertise in CBT, including doctors, nurses and occupational therapists. They will have completed their own professional training and then taken courses to train them to deliver CBT. In view of the relatively small number of qualified psychologists, this must be seen as a positive trend, in that it makes psychological approaches available to many more people.

Accessing Cognitive Behavioural Therapy and other psychological treatment

If you are interested in exploring the possibility of psychological treatment, and you are currently receiving treatment from a Community Mental Health Team or Health Maintenance Organisation, then you can ask your doctor or care worker if such help is available. Otherwise, you can ask your GP or internist about what sort of psychological therapy services are available in your area. These will probably vary from area to area and from country to country. In addition, as with psychiatric help, psychological therapy is also available privately, and in different countries there are official bodies who certify that therapists have the appropriate credentials to offer psychological therapy. CBT is gradually becoming more and more widely available and has proved helpful for a growing variety of psychological and psychiatric problems. Unfortunately this does not mean that you will necessarily find a CBT approach useful in your own life, but it does suggest that it might be worth trying.

At this point we should also mention another group of therapy professionals, Family Therapists. As discussed in chapter 10, the stresses and pressures of family life can exacerbate a variety of psychological problems, and family therapy has been shown to be an effective way of helping sufferers and their families live together more harmoniously. Once again, help can be sought through psychiatric services, your GP or internist or obtained privately.

Psychodynamic psychotherapists and counsellors

The oldest form of psychotherapy, which goes back to Freud, is Psychodynamic Psychotherapy. Unlike CBT, Psychodyamic Therapists are less likely to focus on specific problems and more likely to explore personal relationships, both in the past – looking, for example, at the patient's family history, and in the present – looking closely at the therapy relationship itself. Courses of therapy are usually longer than with CBT.

Psychodynamic Psychotherapy is a large and complicated subject, and one that we do not feel ourselves well qualified to discuss. However, there is not a great deal of research evidence supporting the use of Psychodynamic Psychotherapy with the type of problems that often lead to a diagnosis of schizophrenia. In saying this, we mean no disrespect to those who practise psychodynamic approaches or to patients who have found it beneficial. But we do believe that the research evidence just mentioned makes CBT approaches seem like a better bet for many sufferers.

Psychodynamic Therapists, like Cognitive Therapists, can be doctors, psychologists or members of other professions. They are sometimes attached to community mental health services, but more usually are found in hospital or university departments of psychotherapy. Again, one can also seek psychodynamic therapy privately.

Counsellor is a general term that covers a variety of different theoretical orientations. The counselling profession has become increasingly organised, with professional bodies and well-structured training programmes. Many counsellors, in their training, focus more on the problems experienced by people who do not suffer from specific mental illness, and they may therefore have less experience with people who suffer from schizophrenic-type symptoms. However, a skilled counsellor may well provide a considerable amount of help to someone with such problems, and some sufferers may prefer to deal with a therapist who does not use psychiatric diagnoses. We would suggest, however, that sufferers are careful to check that any counsellor has undergone a reputable training and belongs to an appropriate professional body.

 When Jemma was first ill she asked her GP if she could be referred to a counsellor. However, she was very wary of revealing the real reason for the referral, and in fact did not tell the counsellor about the voices she was hearing. Partly for this reason the counselling sessions were not very helpful for Jemma, and she did not feel that she related well to the counsellor. Fortunately, Jemma had a better experience later in her treatment when she was under the care of her Community Mental Health Team. She saw a psychologist on the team for a few sessions to discuss how to cope with her voices and also attended a voices group; she found both these interventions very helpful.

As Jemma's story illustrates, not every experience with a therapist or counsellor will be helpful. This is because different people have different needs and different models of the kind of help that they might want, and also because a particular patient and therapist may be incompatible as people. If you have had a bad experience of therapy we urge you not to assume that no form of therapy can be helpful to you. There is nothing wrong with 'shopping around' until you find a practitioner whose approach and personality suit you.

Care co-ordinators

Over the last forty years there have been tremendous advances in the treatment of a variety of serious mental illnesses. As a result, it has become increasingly uncommon for sufferers to spend very long periods of time in hospital. Hospital admissions are usually limited to times when the illness is at its worst; more effort has gone into helping sufferers to function in the community. The phrase 'care in the community', called 'de-institution-alisation' in the US, is often used for this change of approach. Newspapers often highlight incidents when the policy of community care does not seem to have worked, but in fact for many people this sort of approach does provide an improved quality of life. As with so much of what we have discussed in this chapter, exact terminology and procedure varies across the world, but one common aspect of this approach is that sufferers who have had many hospitalisations and a severe illness may be monitored while in the community by a care co-ordinator, who is usually a nurse or a social worker. This is again a UK term; terminology and levels of care will vary in different countries, and in the US, from state to state. The care co-ordinator is supposed to meet with the patient regularly, offer them advice and support, and make sure that the patient is staying well, taking medication, and receiving appropriate services. If a patient is receiving various benefits or having financial problems, a care co-ordinator can offer a great deal of practial support. Commonly, the care co-ordinator is also supposed to convene regular meetings of all professionals involved in the patient's care, to keep them informed about any changes in the patient's situation and share information. Another important part of the care co-ordinator's role is often to help the patient access the services of other members of the MDT. For those whose illness is serious and hard to control, and especially those who do not have a supportive partner or family, the help of a good care co-ordinator can be invaluable.

> When Jim was first ill he was assigned a temporary care co-ordinator for a period of about six months. She helped him to sort out some financial problems that had arisen when he was ill and also advised him about practical problems. He later stated that this was very helpful, as it helped him to avoid some of the bad consequences that his illness could have caused.

Other members of the Multi-Disciplinary Team (MDT)

As noted above, particular systems of community care vary from country to country and in the US, from state to state. However, a number of different professional groups are often represented. Social workers can offer advice, support and counselling, and can also help the patient to access various services. Occupational therapists can also work as care co-ordinators, as well as offering training in a variety of skills, ranging from stress management to daily living skills. With the increasing complexity of the Social Security system, many teams employ a Welfare Worker who can advise clients about what they are entitled to and how to obtain it. Resource Workers can advise about courses, charities and other community activities. In many areas, Advocates are becoming increasingly available to patients. They are often volunteers, and sometimes sufferers themselves, and their job is to accompany patients to meetings with professionals to make sure that their views are presented effectively. They can also assist people who want to complain about involuntary detention or any other aspect of their care. Finally, we note that most hospitals employ one or more chaplains, who have experience in talking to mental illness sufferers about how their illnesses may relate to their religious beliefs.

General practitioners

In most countries with a well-developed health care system, patients come to psychiatrists or other mental health workers by way of either a hospital or a General Practitioner (GP; the term 'Internist' is often used in the US). The GP may go by a variety of titles in different countries, but he or she will have a good general knowledge of the symptoms of common illnesses and the sorts of specialists that sufferers should be referred to. Anyone experiencing any sort of mental distress can go to a GP and ask for help and advice. The GP can then refer the patient to a specialist. In addition, there are a number of GPs who have considerable expertise in the field of mental health. Many patients prefer to be treated by their GPs, often in consultation with a psychiatrist, and this can be a very convenient and comfortable arrangement. GPs can certainly prescribe all the necessary medications and order all the necessary tests, especially if a patient is stable on a particular dose of medication, that is, he or she has not fallen ill for some time, and is happy with a particular medication. The most important considerations are that the patient trusts the doctor and that the doctor has enough experience and expertise to feel comfortable in this role.

Support workers

As discussed in chapter 9, many sufferers with long-term mental illness live in hostels and other forms of supported accommodation. Some of these types of accommodation have staff who either live or spend time there, supporting the residents. They may offer practical help and support, as well as emotional support and companionship. Such staff often are without medical or nursing training, but the help they offer can make a big difference in creating a safe and comfortable environment for many sufferers.

Personal relationships with professionals

As we noted above, patients can often feel angry with mental health professionals for a variety of reasons. We also comment that if you feel you have been treated badly, you have a right to make a complaint about any professional. However, it may also happen that you are asked to work with someone whom you dislike. This can be very awkward. The problem is of course not restricted to the area of mental health; you might take a dislike to your butcher, for example. However, you are not forced to go to his shop. By the same token, if you feel you really cannot work with a particular person, you can request a transfer of care. We would like, however, to add a note of caution. Sometimes people take a dislike to their doctor, for example, because she might seem to represent the difficulties and problems of being diagnosed with a mental illness. In such a case, changing doctors might not be very helpful, as the problem could re-occur with your new doctor. On the other hand, if the problem really arises only with this particular person, then a transfer of care might be a very good idea.

As noted above, Simon had a very unpleasant experience when he was first hospitalised. This convinced him that all psychiatrists were cold, unpleasant and arrogant. Fortunately, he had much better experiences during later hospitalisations. His parents were able to play an important

Continued

> role in this, explaining to his doctors what had hap-
> pened to him and how he felt about it. The fact that
> they did this for him also had a positive impact on his
> relationship with them.

Occasionally the opposite problem may arise: some patients may develop strong positive feelings for a particular professional. Perhaps your psychiatrist comes to seem like a wise, understanding father, so that you cannot bear his approaching retirement; perhaps your care co-ordinator is so attractive and caring that you begin to have romantic thoughts about her. This is natural; many professionals may well also be attractive, pleasant people. However, you should bear in mind that all the caring professions have strong professional and ethical prohibitions against the development of personal relationships, and especially intimate relationships, with clients. If you find that such feelings might cause problems with your care, you should probably discuss them with the person involved. Should any professional seem to suggest that they might be interested in a more personal relationship, beware; that person is breaking the ethical code of their profession. He or she could well be banned from practising as a result, and the ensuing problems could well cause great distress to both of you.

Non-professional help: family, friends and support groups

Important as professional help can be, it can often be less important than the support offered by family, friends and other people with similar problems. In chapter 10 we will talk about families, discussing the stresses that family members may experience, but we certainly must emphasise that the family and loved ones can play a crucial role in supporting sufferers. Fellow sufferers can also be very important, and an increasing number of self-help groups are being set up to encourage sufferers to help one another; this is discussed in chapter 8. Finally, good friends can be tremendously important, especially if they are able to listen calmly and with an open mind when sufferers talk about their concerns.

Points covered in this chapter

➡ Psychiatrists are the medical doctors trained to treat serious mental illness; their usual job is to diagnose and prescribe medication.

➡ Clinical Psychologists offer psychological therapies, both through face-to-face treatment and through supervision and consultations. Other members of Multi-Disciplinary Teams will often be trained in the delivery of some forms of psychological treatment.

➡ Cognitive Behavioural Therapy is a form of therapy shown to have a good likelihood of being helpful for people diagnosed with schizophrenia.

➡ A variety of other mental health professionals can offer valuable help with a variety of problems.

➡ If personal feelings like anger or attraction disrupt your relationship with a professional, this is probably best discussed with that person. If such feelings interfere too much, it is probably best to find a new person with whom you can work.

6

The role of medication

Disagreeing about medication

Few things seem as straightforward as the idea that if you have a medical problem, you should go to your doctor and receive a prescription for some helpful medication. However, many medications provoke controversy and disagreement. If a young child behaves badly in school, should he be given medication for hyperactivity, or firm discipline? If a woman is depressed, should she take anti-depressants or just pull herself together? Can childhood vaccinations cause autism? About these and many other issues disagreements can arise and feelings can run high. And certainly many people who have been diagnosed with schizophrenia and their families have conflicting and negative feelings about the medications that are prescribed for it. Why should this be?

Suppose that your life is being made miserable by very noisy neighbours. At every hour of the day and night they scream, shout and play loud music. They also abuse you and shout insults at you when they see you. Now imagine that you complain to the police, and they tell you that you are ill and need to take medication. This medication must be taken regularly, and it has some very unpleasant side effects. It is likely that, in this case, you would feel very insulted, and that even if you did try the medication, you would be unlikely to keep it up for long.

If you have been diagnosed with schizophrenia, this might sound like a familiar scenario. As explained in previous chapters, many people who have been diagnosed with schizophrenia refuse to accept that diagnosis. They may attribute their abnormal experiences to other causes, either external or internal, and in some cases deny altogether having had such experiences. As a result, they may find the suggestion that they should take anti-psychotic medication to be either bizarre or insulting. In addition, as discussed below, these medications may have a variety of unpleasant side effects.

In view of these facts, it is not surprising that many sufferers either reject anti-psychotic medications or are very reluctant to take them. In spite of this, there is a great deal of evidence that many people do benefit from them. In this chapter we will talk about both the benefits and drawbacks of these medications and try to offer some useful advice to sufferers and their families.

Anti-psychotic medication: What is it?

Patients diagnosed with schizophrenia are generally offered a medication from one of the large number of anti-psychotic drugs that are currently available. These drugs are sometimes also referred to as *neuroleptic* drugs or *major tranquillisers*, but we prefer the term 'anti-psychotic' because it makes clear that these drugs are primarily intended to treat the symptoms of psychotic illness. The first anti-psychotic was chlorpromazine (also known as Thorazine in the US and Largactil in the UK), which was discovered in the 1950s; it was initially synthesised as an antihistamine, but was found by chance to relieve the symptoms of psychosis. Before this discovery the only drugs that were generally used to treat psychosis were powerful sedatives, which could calm patients, but had little effect on their symptoms. Lay people often assume that anti-psychotics are primarily intended to sedate patients, but this is not the case. It is true, however, that sedative action is a side effect of many of these medications – in some cases very strong sedative action; this is sometimes helpful but obviously can also create difficulties for many people.

In general, patients diagnosed with schizophrenia or some other psychotic disorder will be started on an anti-psychotic drug. The anti-psychotic effects are not immediate, but generally after a few days or weeks the symptoms of the illness, such as voices, strange beliefs or agitation, will decrease. If they do not, the prescribing doctor may increase the dose of the anti-psychotic or replace it with a different one. As will be discussed below, anti-psychotics can produce a variety of unpleasant side effects, and as a result some patients are not willing to take them for the time necessary to produce positive results; in some cases, this can lead to patients receiving medication involuntarily in hospital. In some cases patients may make a full recovery, with their symptoms disappearing and their lives returning to normal, in which case the anti-psychotic might be reduced and finally stopped. In other cases, depending on the patient's symptoms and past history, he or she might be asked to stay on the medication for a longer period of time to prevent relapse; in such cases the dosage is generally reduced to minimise the side effects. Unfortunately, there are other cases in which the symptoms do not disappear entirely. They may reduce, allowing the patient to function better but still causing some problems; these are referred to as *residual* symptoms.

Finally, there are cases where anti-psychotics do not seem to confer much benefit at all, although these seem to be relatively few in number. The exact mechanism by which anti-psychotics relieve psychotic symptoms is not known. We do know that they work in the spaces between nerve cells, called synapses. The body's nervous system is often compared to the wiring of a telephone system or computer, but unlike the continuous wiring of a telephone exchange, nerve cells have small gaps between them, and the nerve signal is carried across the gap by one of a number of chemicals called *neurotransmitters*, which are produced by one cell and attach themselves to receptors in a neighbouring cell. Many drugs that affect our psychological states work by modifying the action of these neurotransmitters; this is true not only of medications, but also of recreational drugs. Chlorpromazine was discovered to interfere with the action of one neurotransmitter called dopamine and it has also been discovered that some drugs that promote the action of dopamine, including some medications for Parkinson's disease, can cause psychotic symptoms in some people. Further study of neurotransmitters has revealed that the actions of dopamine are complex and varied and that different cells react with it in different ways, and this has led to the development of a variety of different anti-psychotics, as will be discussed in a moment. However, while the evidence suggests that dopamine plays an important part in producing psychotic symptoms, we are not sure exactly why drugs that interfere with the action of dopamine can have a positive effect on psychotic symptoms or what other complex balance of neurotransmitter systems or other factors may be involved.

The anti-psychotics can generally be broken up into four groups. The group discovered first, like chlorpromazine, haloperidol and stelazine, are generally effective but have a variety of side effects, as will be discussed in the next section. A newer group of anti-psychotics, called the *atypical* anti-psychotics, seem to have fewer side effects. *Depot* medication is an anti-psychotic in a long-acting form that can be administered in an injection every two to four weeks. Finally, a lot of attention has been given to an anti-psychotic called *clozapine*. This drug has been found to be very effective, and it can often relieve distress and improve quality of life when other drugs have failed. Unfortunately, it can also cause a dangerous blood disorder. Therefore, people taking it have to have regular blood tests. These tests can pick up any problem before it develops, and, taken in this way, clozapine is safe. Some people find the repeated blood tests unpleasant and off-putting, but we have seen people make dramatic improvements on clozapine; it may well be worth considering if other medications seem to have failed.

Below we include a list of some commonly used anti-psychotics. The list is not complete by any means; new medications are regularly being developed and coming into general use, so no list could be complete. It is also worth noting that usually medications have more than one name. The first name given is their generic name, that is their official medical name, but many drugs are also known by their trade names, the names given by the drug companies. Throughout this chapter the generic name is given first, followed by the trade name, with two names given if the trade name is different in the UK and the US.

DRUGS

Older anti-psychotics: chlorpromazine (Largactil, Thorazine), haloperidol (Haldol), trifluoperazine (Stelazine)

Newer (atypical) anti-psychotics: risperidone (Risperdal), amisulpride (Solian), olanzapine (Zyprexa), clozapine (Clozaril)

Depot medications: flupentixol (Depixol), haloperidol (Haldol decanoate)

Side effects

As explained above, anti-psychotics work by affecting the action of chemical messengers, the neurotransmitters, that are found in the nervous system. Unfortunately, many different parts of the nervous system contain the same neurotransmitters; the result of this is that all of the anti-psychotics do not simply affect psychotic symptoms, but can also cause a number of other, generally unwanted, side effects. For example, we have already mentioned that many of these drugs can have a sedative effect. They are sometimes prescribed to help with sleep or to calm someone who is highly distressed and agitated, but many people understandably find these sedative effects disagreeable. Other side effects can include weight gain, blurred vision, constipation, sensitivity to the sun and apathy or low motivation. These effects vary from drug to drug, and there are many anti-psychotics currently available, so if you are troubled by a particular side effect, it is possible that your doctor can change your medication in an attempt to eliminate it. It is also worth noting that anti-psychotics are not unique in having numerous side effects; all effective medications, including aspirin and vitamin pills, can have unpleasant side effects.

One specific set of side effects is worth a special mention. At about the same time as drug treatments for psychotic disorders were being developed, treatments were also being developed for Parkinson's disease; this is a brain disease that can cause tremor (rapid shaking of the limbs), restlessness, and difficulties in walking and other voluntary movements. In some cases, as noted above, it was found that drugs to treat Parkinson's disease could actually cause psychotic symptoms. Conversely, drugs that block the action of dopamine can produce, usually temporarily, symptoms that are similar to those of Parkinson's disease. These can include restless movement and inability to sit still, or, alternatively, stiffness, lack of mobility, and difficulties in voluntary movement, along with, in some cases, tremor. These symptoms can be controlled by reductions in drug dose, or by so-called anti-Parkinsonian drugs; these are usually prescribed for patients with severe side effects. In a few cases more serious side effects are reported. One of these is *Tardive Dyskinesia*, involuntary movements of the mouth and tongue that persist even when medication is stopped. Fortunately, this illness is not that common and is generally seen in people who have taken the older anti-psychotic drugs for very long periods of time. Finally, occasionally people taking anti-psychotics can show the signs of Neuroleptic Malignant Syndrome, an illness characterised by high fever, muscle stiffness and mental confusion; this is a serious illness and requires medical attention.

Deciding to take anti-psychotics

As we made clear at the beginning of this chapter, many people, having been prescribed anti-psychotic medication, either refuse it, take it only intermittently, or take it with very great reluctance. As we have already suggested, many sufferers simply do not believe that there is anything wrong with them or that their problems can be helped by medication. Many of the side effects that we have just discussed are unpleasant, or sometimes even dangerous, and, for some sufferers, these drugs do not relieve all their symptoms. Further, for many sufferers their introduction to anti-psychotics comes during an involuntary admission to hospital, when they are forced to take medication against their will. Further, accepting medication can be seen as admitting that you are 'a loony', a crazy person who suffers from a stigmatised illness. It is certainly no wonder that many people refuse to take these drugs, in spite of the benefits that they may offer. We also know from research that many people in the general population struggle to take medication as prescribed even for physical illnesses for which there is little evidence of stigma. Is there any way out of this dilemma?

The answer we offer lies in the idea of freedom and autonomy. Most sufferers, most of the time, are not so ill that they have lost the power to decide about medication for themselves. If you are a sufferer, you have perhaps had medication forced upon you, or at the very least felt heavy pressure to take it. Unfortunately, pressure, even from the best of motives, often arouses a negative reaction in the person being pressured. You may therefore be tempted to reject drug treatments out of hand. Although we understand how you might feel, we would suggest a more thoughtful approach. Instead of letting your feelings dictate to you, consider the pros and cons of continued medication. No one can *force* you to take medication over the long term, but many people *choose* to take it because its benefits outweigh its drawbacks. Also, remember that finding the right medication can be a lengthy process. We recommend that you discuss your medication with your doctor and re-evaluate it on an ongoing basis. With any medication, a trial of a month or two could give you some idea of whether or not it improves the quality of your life. If it does not, you can ask your doctor to change it; we have made it clear that there are a wide variety of medications to choose from. Similarly, you may choose not to take medication, and we hope that you will look carefully at how this decision affects the quality of your life as well. The goal should be to control unpleasant experiences and psychological states as much as possible with a minimum of side effects. Patients who work with their doctors to find the best medication for them can often achieve this.

We also suggest that you consider the use of self-monitoring. This simply means devising a form that keeps track of both unpleasant experiences and unpleasant side effects. Ideally, we recommend completing the questionnaire on a weekly basis, with data collected both before and after starting or changing a medication. Looked at over several months, the data collected using such questionnaires could help you form a clearer idea about whether medication is making your life better or not.

When Jemma first sought treatment, she was given one of the older anti-psychotics described above. She found it helped with her voices, but she was especially troubled by weight gain and a sense of tiredness and lack of energy. She and her doctor discussed this and decided to try one of the newer anti-psychotics. Further, before changing the medication, they devised a rating sheet that included both her initial symptoms and the main side effects of the first medication (see Figure 1). Jemma found that most of the ratings improved when she changed her medication, and this helped to confirm for her that the change was beneficial. At a later date she tried reducing her new medication. Again, the rating sheet was helpful, and after a month she decided to go back to her old dose. She found that the fact that her doctor was willing to discuss these changes with her gave her a greater sense of control and willingness to take medication long term. This process of active collaboration in treatment decisions is something that we would regard as crucial to productive relationships between sufferers and therapeutic teams.

	Much Better	A Bit Better	Same	A Bit Worse	Much Worse
Hearing critical voices	☐	☐	☐	☐	☐
Anxiety and restlessness	☐	☐	☐	☐	☐
Weight gain	☐	☐	☐	☐	☐
Can't concentrate	☐	☐	☐	☐	☐
'Things on television are about me'	☐	☐	☐	☐	☐
Trembling hands	☐	☐	☐	☐	☐
'Feeling people are against me'	☐	☐	☐	☐	☐
Tired/no energy	☐	☐	☐	☐	☐

Figure 1. Jemma's personal checklist for medication effectiveness.

If you have found a medication to be reasonably effective at eliminating your symptoms, you may also find yourself with a further dilemma; should you continue to take your medication over a longer term? This is a common problem in many chronic illnesses, such as asthma or diabetes; when people feel reasonably well, they dislike taking medication, and they often either forget to take it or deliberately decide to stop it, even against medical advice. If you are on medication and considering stopping it, we can only urge you to carefully weigh up the risks and benefits. You may be risking illness or hospitalisation, but no one can say for sure what will happen until you actually stop your medication. If you are a family member or caregiver, and someone in your family has stopped their medication and then become ill, please try to be understanding. For all the reasons we have explained, staying on long-term medication is very difficult for many sufferers. Perhaps your loved one needed to try to get by without medication and see what happened. Maybe this experience will help them to reconcile themselves to taking medication over the longer term, if this proves necessary.

Anti-Parkinsonian drugs

As noted above, these are generally given to relieve the side effects of anti-psychotic drugs; they are also called anti-cholinergic drugs. They are not usually prescribed unless side effects like stiffness, rigidity or tremor are reported. It is worth noting that the name of these drugs can cause confusion; anti-psychotic drugs do not cause Parkinson's disease. Instead they can cause side effects that resemble the symptoms of Parkinson's disease, and these drugs treat those side effects.

DRUGS

Anti-Parkinsonian drugs include: procyclidine (Kemadrin), benzat-
ropine (Cogentin), benzhexol/trihexphenidyl (Broflex)
Side effects: Dry mouth, stomach upset, dizziness, blurred vision.
In some cases these drugs may cause a stimulating, mildly
pleasurable effect.

Mood stabilisers

Mood stabilising medications are mainly used in the treatment
of bipolar disorder, also known as manic depression. This disorder generally involves alternating phases of elated and depressed
mood; patients in the elated, or manic, and depressed phases
can experience strange ideas and voices, although these generally seem different from those in patients diagnosed with schizophrenia. However, the dividing line between the two illnesses is
sometimes not that clear, and the diagnosis of schizoaffective
disorder exists for people who do not seem to fall into either
category. For this reason, there are some cases in which patients
diagnosed with schizophrenia are also treated with mood stabilisers. The first mood stabiliser, and the one that is still most
widely used, is lithium; lithium seems to keep many patients in
a stable mood state, helping them to avoid the highs and lows
that normally characterise bipolar disorder. It is, however, very
dangerous in overdose, and regular blood tests are necessary if
you are taking it. Two other mood stabilizers – carbamazepine
and sodium valproate – are also commonly used.

 When Sam first began to experience elated mood, she
was put on lithium. She took it for a while but did not
really like the tremor that it caused in her hands. She

Continued

stopped taking it but later became depressed again. Sam is currently on sodium valproate; she finds that most of the time this will keep her mood stable and help her to avoid both highs and lows. Occasionally, when stressed, her voices will return, and at these times she takes a low dose of olanzapine, one of the newer anti-psychotics.

DRUGS

LITHIUM

Common names: Priadel, Camcolit
Side effects: Increased thirst, dry mouth, tremor. **Note: Lithium can be dangerous in overdose and blood levels need careful monitoring.**

SODIUM VALPROATE

Common names: Epilim, Depakote
Side effects: Nausea, weight gain, tremor

Anti-depressants

Clinical depression has been called 'the common cold of mental illness'; perhaps one person in ten suffers with depression during their lifetime. So-called clinical depression is not simply a bout of 'the blues' but can be a serious illness. Common symptoms of depression include low mood, loss of pleasure and interest in life, poor sleep, guilty thoughts, low self-esteem, and, sometimes, thoughts of suicide or suicide attempts. There are a wide variety of anti-depressant medications. The older anti-depressants, the tricyclics, may be sedating and have a number of other side effects, while the newer serotonin reuptake inhibitors (SSRIs) generally have fewer, different side effects and many people find them easier to take. We list a few here; there are many more and new ones are always coming on the market. It is worth mentioning that all anti-depressants may take between two weeks and a month before they really begin to relieve depression; if you are prescribed one of these drugs, you may have to put up with a period of annoying side effects before you notice any benefit.

Depression can often be triggered by difficult life circumstances, and certainly those who suffer from serious mental illnesses face a variety of difficulties and problems. To suffer from or be diagnosed with a serious illness can be a terrible blow to one's self-esteem, and that diagnosis may also occur in the context of other life problems like job loss, relationship breakdown or problems with education. We will discuss these issues in later chapters and the important role that psychological approaches can have, but we mention them here because studies show that the rate of clinical depression is high in those with the diagnosis of schizophrenia. If you suffer with the symptoms of depression you can certainly discuss the possible benefits and drawbacks of anti-depressant medication with your doctor.

After his second hospitalisation Simon became very depressed for a period of time. He found himself thinking that he had let his parents down and that his life was a failure. He took an anti-depressant for about six months, and this helped to lift his mood and gave him the energy to start to make positive changes in his life.

DRUGS

Tricyclics include: amitriptyline (Lentizol, Elavil) and lofepramine (Gamanil)

Side effects: sedation, dry mouth and constipation. Side effects are worst in the first few weeks after beginning to take these medications.

SSRIs include: fluoxetine (Prozac) and paroxetine (Seroxat, Paxil)

Other new anti-depressants include: venlafaxine (Efexor) and nefazodone (Dutonin)

Side effects: usually less severe than with tricyclics, but do include stomach upset, agitation and rashes. As with tricyclics, side effects are usually at their worst over the first two weeks.

Minor tranquillisers and sleeping pills

These drugs, unlike the anti-psychotics, are true tranquillisers; their main function is to relieve anxiety and cause sleepiness. There was a time when they were very widely prescribed, but they do pose a risk of dependency, some within a relatively short period of time. Agitation and poor sleep are often seen in people with all of the major mental illnesses, and people with a variety of life problems as well. These drugs can offer short-term relief, but they usually do very little to help the problems that are causing poor sleep and agitation, and they can become less effective if used over a long period of time. They are probably best used as short-term treatments, in combination with some other medication that can offer longer-term benefits.

> ## DRUGS
>
> *Minor tranquillisers and sleeping preparations include:* diazepam (Valium), lorazepam (Ativan), alprazolam (Xanax) and zopiclone (Zimovane). These drugs can reduce anxiety and improve sleep in the short term but there is a danger of dependency

A last word

As we hope we have made clear, the whole issue of medication for serious mental illness is a complex and difficult one. It has many difficulties and problems associated with it, but we do believe that many people can benefit from treatment with medication. At the same time, it is far from being the whole answer and there are some people for whom a balanced review of the evidence indicates that it is not beneficial. We believe that attention to psychological and social factors is also very important in helping sufferers, and we hope to make this clearer later in this book.

Points covered in this chapter

➡ Some sufferers dislike taking anti-psychotic drugs for a variety of reasons. Many of these reasons are understandable and are similar to the reasons reported by people prescribed medication for physical health problems. However, anti-psychotic medication can also be very helpful for many sufferers.

➡ Anti-psychotic drugs are not a cure for psychotic symptoms, but they can relieve them either completely or partially for the great majority of sufferers.

➡ Unfortunately anti-psychotic drugs may have a number of unpleasant side effects. Some of these side effects can be relieved by taking anti-Parkinsonian medication, or by changing medication or reducing doses.

➡ Mood stabilisers are not routinely given to those diagnosed with schizophrenia, but they can be helpful in some cases.

➡ Anti-depressants are an effective treatment for most cases of depression, and depression can be one effect of the difficulties associated with the diagnosis of schizophrenia.

➡ Minor tranquillisers do not treat the symptoms of schizophrenia but they can be useful in treating insomnia and anxiety. They are best not taken for long periods of time as there is a risk of dependency.

7

Cognitive Behavioural Therapy

Background

This chapter describes a form of psychological treatment known as Cognitive Therapy. This approach can also be referred to as Cognitive Behavioural Therapy, a term which is often shortened to CBT. Other psychological approaches exist, but this chapter focuses on CBT because there is now a substantial body of scientific evidence that supports its effectiveness and it is the form of treatment with which the authors have the most clinical experience and expertise. The reader is encouraged to refer to this chapter for information on this psychological approach and for indications of possible useful strategies based on it. It should be emphasised, however, that we are not proposing 'do it yourself' therapy. It is necessary to work with a skilled therapist if you decide you want to work on your problems in a detailed CBT manner. Many of the clinicians who provide this form of treatment are Clinical Psychologists, but increasingly nurses and psychiatrists are training in CBT skills. This chapter therefore has two aims: first, to provide information on a useful psychological approach that you may well be able to access through referrals by your psychiatrist or General Practitioner; and second, if such professional help is not currently available, to provide some practical suggestions that you might wish to employ independently. A further issue that it is important to bear in mind is that people differ widely on the elements of therapy that they find most useful in addressing their particular problems. This should be not be a surprise, as, of course, all people are different and this applies whether you happen to have a diagnosis of schizophrenia, or anxiety, or no diagnosis at all. It is therefore helpful to read this chapter from the perspective of a scientist, experimenting with suggestions until you find those that you regard as most useful for you.

What is Cognitive Behavioural Therapy (CBT)?

CBT is a form of psychological treatment that focuses on looking at the connections between thoughts, feelings and behaviour. A Cognitive Therapist will often obtain information on how problems might have developed, but the main targets of treatment will be on changing things in the present. This approach was first developed around fifty years ago in response to dissatisfaction with other psychological treatments. It was first used with problems such as depression and anxiety. Many scientific studies have demonstrated the effectiveness of this approach for these disorders, but it has only been applied to schizophrenia more recently. Indeed A.T. Beck, who originally developed CBT, initially believed that schizophrenia was probably the one disorder in which his therapeutic approach might not be helpful. His view changed when encouraging research findings began to be reported in this area and indeed he is actively involved in developing this approach currently.

Until the late 1980s there were very few reports of CBT being used with people with a diagnosis of schizophrenia. When this approach was first proposed some clinicians were quite resistant to it, believing that talking in detail about the symptoms of schizophrenia could make them worse. Others thought that schizophrenia had mainly physical causes and therefore that treatments other than medication were unlikely to be helpful. This situation has changed significantly in recent years. There is now clear evidence that people with schizophrenia can benefit significantly from CBT and that it is an approach that is highly valued.

In CBT the therapist and client collaborate to explore thoughts, feelings and behaviour. This can include quite detailed work considering how patterns of thoughts, feelings and behaviour have evolved over time and what functions they have served for the individual.

They then work out together how these three areas might interconnect for this individual and what patterns might be associated with the problems that the individual might be working on. Although the focus of this approach is to help people to deal with problems that they are currently experiencing, it does not mean that the past is ignored. It is part of a CBT approach to develop a detailed history of relevant events and experiences from the client's perspective. This information is often crucial in identifying and understanding the patterns of current thoughts and beliefs that might be associated with distress.

This approach therefore emphasises client and therapist working together with recognition of expertise on both sides. The therapist has experience and expertise in the CBT approach, whilst clients have expertise in their own experiences. It is only by bringing together the expertise of both sides that effective treatment can be provided.

Simon first had experience of hallucinations when he was twelve years old. He had enjoyed seeing friendly creatures come to his room and felt both fascinated and protected by them. They appeared each night in his room and sat on his bed. He never discussed these experiences with anyone else, including his parents, as he wanted them to be his secret. These experiences stopped after a couple of years and he initially thought little more of them. However, when he began to feel unsettled he dwelt on the meaning that he attached to these experiences and began to become preoccupied with the idea that more sinister creatures from other worlds would come and harm him and the people close to him. He thought back to things he thought these creatures had said and felt that this had special and sinister significance. These concerns had not been expressed before he began CBT, although he had been receiving psychiatric treatment for some years. He said that he hadn't told anyone previously because he was concerned about how they would react but also, because it had happened a while ago and had felt pleasant at the time, he had thought it probably was not relevant to his current difficulties. He and his psychologist were then able to explore how this developing pattern of beliefs and experiences might have served some important functions for him at that time in his life. It seemed that these experiences began at a time in Simon's life when he felt particularly vulnerable and afraid and that initially they helped him cope with other difficulties that he was experiencing in everyday life. They also explored whether some of the beliefs that developed at that time might still be operating currently in relation to the more distressing experiences he was currently reporting.

Continued

This is a good example of the importance of both client and therapist pooling their knowledge. The client alone had expertise in his own range of experiences while the psychologist was able to use psychological knowledge to integrate these experiences in ways that eventually made sense to both of them and indicated some appropriate targets for psychological treatment approaches.

The importance of what we do

The things we do (our behaviours) are extremely important in relation to how we think and what we feel. An important aim for most people is to achieve a balance in the range and type of activities that we engage in. As will be discussed below, both doing too much and doing too little can cause people to feel worried, bored or distressed. Many people with a diagnosis of schizophrenia, for instance, will have been informed at some time or other that their illness can be made worse by stress. This information is often conveyed with the best of intentions and there certainly is evidence that if people have significant events that are difficult to cope with, then they can be more at risk of becoming unwell than if life is going smoothly. However, if the term 'stress' is not properly explained, the individual can be left with a concern that anything that they do could lead to illness. Stress is in fact neither a good thing nor a bad thing. Some stress is involved in almost all conscious activity. Reading, writing, driving, walking, playing sports or computer games, attending classes or going to work all involve some stress. Research also indicates that in the right amounts some stress can be helpful. People experiencing moderate levels of stress often have better concentration and higher levels of performance than people who are totally relaxed. An example of this is with sportsmen and women, who will often rely on adrenalin to help them to compete at high levels of performance.

However, stress does cause problems when it becomes strain. That is when the amount of stress being experienced outstrips your ability to deal with it. Thus, small amounts of even quite intense stress can often be coped with if they are then followed by periods of calm when the system can recover. Also, the amount of stress that can be coped with will depend on how you are feeling. If you are feeling relaxed, positive and strong then it would usually take a high level of stress to cause you problems, if however you are feeling tired, vulnerable and in low spirits then it is likely that smaller amounts of stress may cause problems.

If people have been told that stress is bad for them, without proper explanation, they can avoid almost all activities and become isolated and withdrawn. This can be a source of stress in its own right and actually begin to cause the problems that the person was trying to solve. If you have a range of activities that give you access to a range of people and experiences, then on average this will tend to be associated with feeling better. People who are chronically under-active and isolated, whether they have a psychiatric diagnosis or not, will tend to have poorer mood than those who have a balance of activities and periods of relaxation. Therefore, the things we do can affect both mood and stress levels.

Learning relaxation skills

It is possible to learn skills in relaxation. These skills can be helpful for anyone, but are especially useful if you are dealing with the stress and strains of everyday life and are also trying to manage a mental health problem. Deep muscle/applied relaxation approaches were used with Jim below, with some success. The detailed protocol for this approach is presented in Appendix 2.

Jim was experiencing strain in his relationship with Rachel. When they had disagreements he felt wound up and thought that the only way of dealing with this was to get things off his chest. Unfortunately, this often led to Rachel being upset and to further arguments. Jim wanted to find a different way of dealing with this. He and his psychologist therefore began a programme of applied relaxation. Jim learnt how to achieve a deep state of relaxation through this programme and was able to use his skills when he started to feel tense or wound up. This helped him to approach his discussions in a calmer manner, which was beneficial for both Jim and Rachel.

Not everyone finds that particular form of relaxation helpful. There are other alternatives and one that Jemma found beneficial was mindfulness relaxation. This is based on clearing the mind through diaphragmatic breathing to allow you to focus more on the present than on worries or anticipated problems. The script for this approach is, again, presented in Appendix 2.

Jemma tried deep muscle relaxation but did not like it. She wanted to try to calm herself before college, but found that this approach was not right for her. She and her psychologist looked at possible reasons for this and decided to try an alternative approach. Instead of deep muscle relaxation Jemma learnt skills in mindfulness relaxation. In this approach she learnt to focus on her breathing and to practise allowing her worrying thoughts to pass through her mind, without undue attention. This technique does not require the participant to aim for a particular state of relaxation, which can be helpful as

Continued

> some people find that trying to relax can paradoxically lead to increased tension. She found that, although this technique specifically states that you are not trying to relax as such, by practising regularly she felt significantly calmer.

In terms of activities it can be helpful to look at what patterns of behaviour you are currently involved in. Often a psychologist would suggest that you keep a diary of what you are doing over a period of a couple of weeks. This would then be discussed to look at patterns and to find out how you felt about the things you were doing. Quite often it becomes clear from looking at these diaries that a person might benefit from making some changes in their patterns of behaviour. These changes can then be tested out to see if they have the desired effect.

Thus, if a person is staying at home all week and doing very little, it could be seen whether a gradual increase in activity outside the house led to improvements in mood. Such a change often does lead to mood improvements and indeed people with depression often also benefit from the same approach. Similarly, if you save your energy for chores and other practical tasks, but then have no energy for recreational activities, this will not be helpful. Often people then report feeling more and more tired and may then feel they have to try harder, so that a vicious circle develops. It can be important to plan ways to still get the major tasks done but also have space for things that are positive and enjoyable. The essential message here is that everyone needs a balance of activities and rest, chores and fun. If we are aware of feeling unwell then it may be a sign to do less temporarily but opting out should not then develop into a chronic pattern.

People with a diagnosis of schizophrenia sometimes also find that they avoid or engage in particular activities for reasons other than stress. Particular beliefs concerning threats from others or expectations of disaster may also lead to withdrawing from life. This withdrawal may then reinforce such beliefs because *avoiding* risky situations means that you never find out how accurate these concerns were. This can then lead to further withdrawal that can lower mood and increase distress.

The importance of what we think

Thinking is the process by which we make sense of the experiences that we are currently having and those that have occurred in the past. Thinking is used to plan what we will do in the future and to assess risks in our environment and how to avoid them. Thoughts are fundamental processes and occur at numerous levels. Conscious thoughts are thoughts that we are actively aware of thinking. However, there are other thoughts that occur regularly of which we are less aware: these are called 'automatic thoughts' and are mental reflexes in response to particular situations. Having automatic thoughts is perfectly normal and is in fact crucial for normal functioning. If every action had to be analysed by conscious thought we would not be able to engage in even a small percentage of our normal activities; we would spend all our time thinking instead of doing. These automatic thoughts are therefore usually helpful.

However, problems can occur when these thoughts go awry. Negative automatic thoughts happen when, through past experiences or through events in childhood, the person sees certain aspects of themselves or the world around them in a negative light. When thoughts of this type are regularly triggered by events it can be emotionally very painful. Within CBT an important aspect of therapeutic work can be for therapist and client to identify these thoughts. This is important because most thoughts of this type are gross exaggerations or distortions of the truth. When they have been identified they can be analysed and tested to find out whether they are helpful and accurate. If they are not, then such thoughts may need to be amended to better reflect what is actually happening in the external world. If these thoughts are not addressed they tend to continue to be automatic and have their effect often without you being directly aware of them. Thus, if a range of situations triggered off a thought 'I am not safe' you might usually be aware of feeling fear and wanting to avoid those situations. If this continued then the thought itself might never be evaluated. By working together with a therapist to capture these thoughts, it can then be possible to test them out.

The process of identifying and testing thoughts can be a powerful one. People who do this are often able, over time, to develop more helpful thoughts to replace previous automatic ones and reduce distress.

Simon kept a thought record for situations when he was in town. He found that he was aware of feeling very unsafe in town, even during the day, but was unsure why. He began to take very brief trips into town and to note the thoughts he was having when he began to feel unsafe and scared. His thoughts included 'they are laughing at me', 'they are pointing at me', 'they will hit me'. Initially Simon worked with his therapist on evaluating these thoughts within a session. It appeared that they stemmed from a couple of experiences that Simon had some years ago when he was becoming ill. He had at that time been homeless for two short periods and on both occasions had been subjected to verbal and physical abuse by groups of youths. These understandably distressing experiences seemed to have triggered these thoughts, which still occurred many years afterwards and in very different situations.

Continued

Simon was also able to observe that when in town he made sure not to look at anyone but just rushed through, anxious to get out and home. He therefore never got to see whether people's reactions were not as he felt them to be. He and his therapist visited town on two occasions, during which Simon agreed to make a conscious effort to notice the people around him and their behaviour. He found that people were in fact paying very little attention to him and that the shouts and laughter he heard were people involved in conversations which were unconnected with him. As he explored his thoughts it became possible for him to begin to challenge them and eventually to amend them. He continued to be appropriately cautious about being out at 'risky times' such as late at night, but became much more comfortable using the shops and other facilities during the normal shopping hours. His experience of doing this more frequently in the absence of assault or other harmful consequences then served to support his increased confidence in his less negative automatic thinking.

The importance of our feelings

The other area that is central to a CBT approach is feelings or emotions. People usually come to seek help for mental health problems because of the feelings that they are having. Although thoughts can be troublesome and behaviour can lead to problems, it is usually only if the person feels distress that they will seek help. This is just as true of people with a diagnosis of schizophrenia, as it is of any of the other mental health difficulties that any of us might experience. Feelings are not, however, only important when they are a sign of illness or distress. How we feel will often be very important in guiding what we do and how we react to situations. If a person runs, shouting and waving, towards you, it might cause you to feel fear; if you felt fearful you might have thoughts about needing to protect yourself or run away. Then you might also be aware of adrenalin pumping and your heart speeding up as you prepared either to fight or run from the potential threat. If however the person running towards you was doing this while wearing a clown's outfit and you were aware that this was a carnival day event, then the same behaviour might cause different feelings, possibly of alarm, followed by surprise and then possibly amusement. These different emotional reactions would be associated with different evaluations of the situation and also of the potential threat posed. How we feel can affect both how we react to situations, but also what we do more routinely. Thus, if you are aware of feeling tired and rather low your feelings will usually indicate that you need to do less, rest and wait until you feel more like being active again. This reaction can be very helpful if the reason for this tiredness is a cold or flu bug. However, if the reason is to do with thoughts and feelings it is less helpful. With psychological reactions, if you respond to tiredness and low mood by waiting for things to pass, the mood has a tendency to get lower, and doing less can often be associated with feeling more, rather than less, tired. In this sort of situation feelings are not a good guide to action. Rather it can be important to engage in moderate levels of activity that tend to help mood and then often feelings of fatigue will reduce.

Within CBT a lot of effort is put into understanding the links between thoughts, feelings and behaviour. Identifying these relationships can help you to be alert to when your feelings are serving your best interest and when they are not.

Jemma found that although she wanted to learn more about computing she was not managing to get to the classes she had enrolled for at her local college. She said that she would go when she felt better, but was disappointed when, over several weeks, it appeared that her feelings hadn't changed. Her feelings were of tiredness and anxiety, which seemed to confirm to her that she could not go to college. She initially thought that unless she was feeling very calm and positive she would not be able to learn anything and that the course would be a waste of time. She identified a conflict between a strong wish to go to this course and a feeling that she should not. Within therapy it was possible to look at this feeling and to explore the thoughts and behaviours associated with it. It became clear that the less she attended, the worse this feeling got. It was therefore agreed between Jemma and her therapist that she would try to focus on her goal of attending the course and monitor whether her feelings changed over time. As noted previously, Jemma was able to learn relaxation skills which were helpful in feeling that she had some control over her anxieties. Jemma was then able to collect evidence that with regular attendance she did make progress, even when feeling a bit below par, and also that the combination of meeting with new people and learning were actually associated with more energy and less anxiety as the course progressed. Jemma reported feeling very positive about this experience, as it indicated to her that she had some control and could make choices, rather than being dictated to by her illness and the feelings associated with it, which she had felt previously to be the case.

Understanding upsetting thoughts and experiences

Many people with a diagnosis of schizophrenia have experiences that are distressing. These may be visions, voices, intrusive thoughts or upsetting beliefs. These experiences in their own right can be very difficult to cope with, but are made worse by the widely held belief that they are alone in having these experiences. Many people with a diagnosis of schizophrenia can find discussing their experiences with people in similar situations extremely powerful, as it can help them to discover that they are not alone. It is important to point out that many people without a diagnosis of schizophrenia will have experience to a greater or lesser extent with 'schizophrenic symptoms'. Thus, there are many examples of people under extreme stress (for instance through anxiety, bereavement or drug problems) who experience hallucinations. It is therefore important that people with this diagnosis understand that their experiences are not incomprehensible 'madness', but are often quite logically connected to patterns of experiences that they had had earlier in their lives. This means that it is seen as important in CBT to develop a detailed account of each person's experiences as they are happening in the present and also how they have developed over time. Often, collecting this information can indicate how experiences originated and also what things seem to be important in making them more or less likely to occur in the present. This can then allow people to work towards gaining greater control of these experiences, which increases confidence and tends to reduce distress and feelings of powerlessness, which can be common among people who are living with a longstanding mental health problem.

Many people report that an important aspect of working with a therapist is being able to talk about things that they experience as real and to have the opportunity of discussing the implications of these experiences. This will often be in contrast with previous experiences of either having their beliefs directly challenged or sometimes ignored by others, who find them strange or frightening.

Taking control through thought challenges and experiments

An important aspect of CBT approaches is that no one assumes that they know the truth. Everyone has beliefs, some of which will be true and some will be false. Equally, some beliefs will be helpful, whereas others will tend to cause significant problems in everyday life. Therefore, once it is clearer what your beliefs might be and how they might have developed it can often be useful to investigate and test out beliefs that appear to be causing distress. This is not the same as saying that a therapist should tell you what it is reasonable to believe. A key feature of this approach is that clients use a questioning approach to work out for themselves which beliefs are helpful. This can be done by people investigating evidence in relation to particular thoughts and beliefs, or in relation to the impact of such beliefs. Exploring this with the support of a psychologist can lead to powerful changes that can be very helpful for the individual. This approach is in contrast to a more traditional medical view of 'unusual beliefs' as symptoms of illness whose content is of little significance.

 Jim believed that other people could access his mind. He believed that a large number of people locally were able to tap into his thoughts and that often they would then discuss the thoughts that they had observed. Understandably, Jim found this distressing, but had over the years managed to cope with this in many situations by distracting himself. However, he found that when he was in noisier places, like his local pub, the belief got

Continued

stronger and would disturb his concentration when he was playing darts for the local team. When he was with Rachel he found that whenever they hugged or kissed he felt as though this also was public and therefore was less physically affectionate than he would have liked to be, which put some strain on their relationship. Jim agreed in therapy to test out a particular aspect of his belief. He said that part of the evidence for his belief that people could tap into his thoughts was that he often heard parts of these thoughts repeated in crowded places. Jim tested this out by working out a range of uncommon thoughts (such as thinking in French, a language with which he was familiar) and recording how often these thoughts were repeated when he was out playing darts. As he was understandably nervous, he used the relaxation skills, referred to earlier, in this situation to help him cope, prior to testing out his beliefs. He found that it was only commonly used words that appeared to be repeated. When this evidence was discussed he felt that the extent to which his thoughts were being monitored was rather less than he had previously believed. He also decided that even if some monitoring had been going on, this had been happening for ten years without any significant consequences. He therefore decided that he felt reasonably safe to ignore it and chose for himself how he behaved. This led to greater closeness with Rachel and helped reduce the strain that there had been on their relationship.

Changing the things you do – routine and reward

Although many people talk about the importance of freedom and spontaneity, in fact most of us function best when we are working with a certain degree of routine. This does not mean that people need to do the same things, at the same time, every day. However, when people's activities and environment are unpredictable over long periods of time it is common for them to experience symptoms of strain such as tension, anxiety, low mood and fatigue. There is evidence for this from people who do shift work, people who undertake regular air travel and people who lose out on routine because of losing or changing employment. It is therefore important to have some form of structure for regular activities, to reduce the likelihood of symptoms of strain and to optimise psychological health. In practice this would mean not having bed and wakening times that generally vary by more than an hour or so over a week. It would also be helpful to avoid long periods of inactivity and to have some sort of plan for conducting daily tasks. An advantage of taking this practical approach is that planning ahead can allow you to plan for pleasant and interesting activities as well as tasks. All of us need some rewards and although we would like other people to recognise our efforts, this can be a little unpredictable. The one person who should always be aware of what we are doing is oneself: by considering what you are doing you can also think about how you will reward yourself for completing tasks.

 Jemma found it very hard to keep her garden manageable. She had spent some years looking for a flat with a small garden and had been thrilled when this was offered to her. However, she found that when she moved in, her time was taken up with other things and that now the garden was overgrown with weeds. When she looked out at it her heart sank as she felt that it would take ages to sort it out and she doubted she had the energy to do it. However, she found that not having done this made her feel low, frustrated and disappointed, so she wanted

Continued

to find some way out of the log jam. It was agreed therefore to plan to spend thirty minutes each day, and no more, in the garden. This was a length of time that Jemma was confident she could spare and with which her energy levels could cope.

For each time period a small task was identified so that there would be evidence of concrete progress for her efforts. It was also planned that she would, after two weeks of this work, take a trip to a forthcoming garden show to reward herself for her efforts and to maintain her enthusiasm. Working in this way she got her garden under control in a couple of weeks and then spent several more weeks buying and putting in plants that she liked. This then became a pleasant space in which she could relax rather than one that was full of unpleasant chores, to which she had to attend in addition to her other daily tasks.

Building on current coping skills

We know that many people with a diagnosis of schizophrenia have in fact got excellent coping skills. It never ceases to impress us how people who are living with the most terrifying experiences continue on with productive lives and relationships. This alone is a testament to the strength of character and resourcefulness of many people with mental health problems. One of the tasks in CBT will therefore often involve building on, and making more systematic, the coping skills that people have already developed for themselves. Research has shown that often people might use a helpful strategy erratically or in combination with other approaches that are less helpful. A process of testing out coping approaches can help to refine the skills used to maximise their effectiveness.

Sam initially felt that there was nothing she could do when she felt her mood becoming lower. However, on discussion with her psychologist she noted that she had on two occasions spent some time with her close friend Helen when she was feeling low. She had found that on those occasions, although she had not enjoyed Helen's company as much as usual, her mood had not gone any lower and had actually gradually improved. Having identified one approach, Sam gained confidence and was eventually able to produce a checklist of effective coping approaches. This was important both in reducing the impact of further mood episodes and increasing Sam's sense of control over the course of her problems.

Catching things before they get worse

Psychological techniques are best learnt when things are not in crisis. When skills have been learnt and applied they can be very powerful in reducing the impact of symptoms and in reducing the risk of becoming unwell again in the future. An important aspect of staying well, which CBT emphasises, is being knowledgeable about your own mental health. Most of us assume we know what being well is, but we don't. Being well or 'normal' is different for different people. Essentially a state of 'wellness' is when we are without significant signs of emotional distress and are able to work towards our major goals in life, without psychological problems significantly interfering with this. To work out what 'well' means for each person requires that person to become familiar with his or her moods and what affects them, both for better and for worse. Monitoring this can be very important because then you can have early warnings of any mood changes. The research shows that when people with a diagnosis of schizophrenia pick up and act to correct early changes in mood or symptoms they can often achieve this by using cognitive or behavioural strategies. These can then significantly reduce the likelihood of mood or symptom changes worsening or getting to the point of requiring increased psychiatric treatment.

Family therapy

Family relationships can be put under great strain by the experience of schizophrenia. People who are living with this diagnosis will often struggle to understand their experiences and therefore not always be readily able to explain their reactions and behaviour to those around them. There are therefore many opportunities for misunderstanding to develop and the potential for strain within families and between couples. Again, there is research evidence that psychological approaches can have important benefits for individuals and families where this is an issue. Clearly, if an individual is able to make progress with a CBT approach this may indirectly be of benefit to others, but it is often helpful to work with the family as a whole. A short summary of some of the issues involved in family therapy is presented below. This is dealt with in more detail in chapter 10.

There is a substantial amount of research now that indicates that family therapy, or Cognitive Behavioural Family Therapy, can have important effects on both the attitudes of family members and the mental health of individuals with a diagnosis of schizophrenia. The focus of this work will usually be on helping families to reach a shared understanding of the experiences that the individual is dealing with. On the basis of this they then work towards patterns of support and communication that are helpful both to the person with a diagnosis of schizophrenia and to the family as a whole. Although information provided to families and caregivers is gradually improving they will often have had little information when their family member became ill. Even when information has been provided there is also a need to support caregivers in terms of their own emotional reactions to the problems which their partner or relative is experiencing. While some people can become very critical of the individual with this diagnosis, others can become critical of themselves for not being able to rescue their loved one from the problems that they are experiencing. A key task therefore within this approach is to work with all those involved to try to find a balance between their needs and the needs of others. A positive outcome of this approach is when families develop a shared view of the mental health issues around the diagnosis of schizophrenia. This can allow them to work together towards addressing difficulties, while also being able to capitalise on positive aspects of recovery.

Social contacts and support

As noted earlier in the chapter, some people initially tend to withdraw from social contact and activities outside the home. However, having a range of social contacts is important for all of us. Some of these may be accessed through the day services of your local mental health service but there are also a range of self-help and voluntary groups, which might be important sources of support and social contact. These include MIND, Hearing Voices Network, Making Space and Survivors network in the UK, and the National Alliance for the Mentally Ill and Schizophrenics Anonymous in the US. This is considered in detail in chapter 8.

Points covered in this chapter

➡ This chapter describes a psychological treatment approach known as Cognitive Behavioural Therapy (CBT), which the authors have clinical experience of applying to people with a diagnosis of schizophrenia.

➥ CBT is delivered in conjunction with a qualified therapist but there are aspects of therapy that may be tried out independently.

➥ CBT explores the relationships between thoughts, feelings and behaviour and concentrates on making changes in the present.

➥ CBT is effective for a range of mental health problems including depression and anxiety.

➥ Research over the last fifteen to twenty years has demonstrated that CBT can have significant benefits for people with a diagnosis of schizophrenia.

➥ CBT is based on therapist and client working together to identify unhelpful patterns of behaviour and thought. They will often explore how these patterns might have developed historically and what functions they might have served in the past.

➥ Client and therapist work together to discuss alternative helpful behaviour or thought patterns. This will be based on both the therapist's skills in CBT and the client's skills and knowledge with respect to their own experiences.

➥ An important aspect of a CBT approach is generating a shared account of an individual's experiences as understandable and therefore potentially controllable. This is helped by an awareness of a continuum of experiences in the general population that share much in common with experiences reported by people with a diagnosis of schizophrenia.

➥ No one knows the absolute truth, therefore change occurs in CBT through agreed challenges and experiments. These are developed through mutual agreement and can be very powerful in increasing the client's confidence in his or her own coping skills.

➡ Some elements of routine are helpful for most of us, including people who have a diagnosis of schizophrenia. This includes making time for practical tasks, but also ensuring a balance between this and relaxation/recreation.

➡ Effective psychological help often involves recognising and building on the effective coping strategies that people have had to learn to help them live with their particular difficulties. Sometimes it also involves identifying approaches that have been used only occasionally and making them a more central part of the individual's set of coping strategies.

➡ CBT skills are best learnt when not in a crisis. They can help in identifying when problems are developing and provide the individual with ways of acting to reduce the likelihood of such problems escalating into episodes of illness.

➡ The main focus of the chapter is on individual CBT, however it is recognised that the impact of schizophrenia goes beyond the individual to families, friends and colleagues.

➡ Family therapy uses a combination of CBT and psychoeducational approaches, working with individual clients and key relatives. There is again substantial research evidence to indicate the effectiveness of this approach.

➡ In addition to formal therapeutic interventions, more informal social contacts are very important. These can be supported through mental health services, but also through voluntary agencies and self-help groups.

8

Importance of self-help in dealing with issues associated with schizophrenia

Connections between self-help and psychological approaches

Self-help fits well with a psychological approach to mental health problems in general and schizophrenia in particular. Although people are occasionally overtaken by their problems to the extent that they may need inpatient support, for the vast majority of the time people living with schizophrenia live largely independent lives. Even individuals who experience several episodes of illness will often be able to cope quite well in between these. This means that the thoughts and views of people with life experience of schizophrenia on how to cope with mental health problems are clearly valuable and can be of considerable benefit to those who have similar problems, as well as to the quality of their own care. It is often the case that the experiences that people have

109

had, and how they have dealt with them, have informed developments in treatment approaches. In particular, the coping skills and difficulties that people have reported during the course of CBT treatments have been important in shaping the structure of the psychological approaches that people receive.

Self-help is a broad term and can mean different things to different people. Some individuals find that group activities are extremely helpful and important in helping them to cope, others may find them unpleasant and difficult to cope with. Just as with CBT or the prescription of medication, a 'one size fits all' approach will not work. It is again a matter of taking a scientific approach to identifying what actually works best for you as an individual. For some people self-help can mean engaging in a range of activities that have nothing to do with mental illness specifically, but which they know from experience can help them maintain their own optimal level of functioning. Equally, other people may find that they prefer to read books or other informative material to supplement any professional help that they are receiving. Any of these approaches can have merit and for many people it is a process of trial and error to identify which are the most beneficial for them.

The increasing importance of self-help groups

Over the last ten to fifteen years there has been a substantial expansion in the number and also the influence of self-help groups. Appendix 1 provides a list and contact details of some of the larger groups in the UK (including MIND, Hearing Voices Network, Survivors Network) and the US (including the National Alliance for the Mentally Ill and Schizophrenics Anonymous). Although there were self-help groups prior to this, they were often more related to the needs of caregivers than users of services. Often they were strongly linked to psychiatric services and embraced broadly psychiatric models of illness.

However, this left a large number of service users without representation, especially those who are sceptical about their experience of the psychiatric system.

There are now numerous groups run and developed by users, which have a range of roles from political lobbying to individual support. The influence of the user movement is something that has been acknowledged both in the UK and the US. Legislation now routinely emphasises the importance of user involvement both in the development of policy and in the development and running of services. There is also now recognition that research into the causes and treatments of mental health problems should have significant input from the people who are likely to be consumers of such treatments. It is again important to recognise that this process is at an early stage and is not perfect. There can be a risk of tokenism in which people who use mental health services are given access to research or management meetings but without the support or infrastructure to allow them to make a full contribution. There is greater awareness, often as a result of the efforts of these groups, of the importance of providing people with information, training and payment in order to recognise their professional contributions in an appropriate manner.

A characteristic of more recent groups is that they identify their experiences as being of value even if associated with distress (rather than being merely expressions of insanity). This has led to proposals for living with symptoms of illness in ways that allow other life goals to be met, rather than putting life on hold until full symptom relief or suppression is achieved through medication or other means. This approach again is consistent with psychological views of the symptoms associated with a diagnosis of schizophrenia. In particular, as noted in chapter 3 and elsewhere, a key issue for many people is as much the meaning and interpretation of psychotic experiences as their existence as such.

What self-help groups do

Advocacy

Many self-help organisations have an advocacy role as part of their activities. Advocates can be people with or without a history of mental health problems themselves, who are aware of some of the issues that people with a diagnosis of mental illness might routinely face. When an individual with a mental health problem has difficulties in communicating, either with people within mental health services or with other agencies, an advocate can be a valuable asset. The reasons for communication problems can be diverse. Sometimes an individual may feel the need for an advocate for moral support in a potentially difficult meeting, at other times it may be that the person currently feels too emotionally fragile to take the lead in a discussion that they would normally be able to cope with. Experienced advocates will often have access to information regarding legislation and service provision requirements that can be of benefit to service users.

Help and support with practical issues can also come from other agencies. Social services can provide help and advice with respect to financial, housing and benefits issues. In the UK the Citizens Advice Bureau also provides valuable services in advising individuals on financial, legal, housing and employment matters.

 Jim was concerned because he had fallen behind with his rent. Although he normally paid this regularly he had missed several weeks when he had been unwell. His landlord had given him a relatively short period of time to repay this debt and Jim was worried that he would not manage to do so. He was becoming increasingly worried that this might put his home under threat. He found out about his local Citizens Advice Bureau and asked for their

Continued

help. They were able to help him work out a repayment plan and to write a very clear letter to his landlord setting out his previous good payment history and a realistic timescale for paying off the debt. Jim found to his relief that, although his landlord was not pleased that the timescale was slightly longer than his original deadline, he accepted the repayment plan. This allowed Jim to concentrate on keeping to this plan and removed the stress of anticipating possible homelessness.

Therapy/counselling

The main form of psychological therapy described in this book is CBT. This is the approach used by the authors and is supported by scientific research. However, not everyone feels it is for them and even people who do may not always be able to access it. There are a number of self-help groups that offer counselling services both in groups and for individuals. These range from relatively informal sessions to structured psychotherapy. In addition, it is now possible to access alternative therapies (such as massage, aromatherapy, yoga) through some self-help groups and through some day hospital services. Although from a scientific point of view there is little evidence for alternative therapies as a particular treatment for schizophrenia, there is little doubt that many people value them. Our perspective is that both people with and without a mental health history find many of these approaches leading to a 'feel good' factor and without evidence of any significant risks. Since 'feeling good' is important to all of us, we see no reason why reputable alternative approaches cannot be part of an overall approach to recovery.

Support and validation

The presence of the user-self-help movement has had important non-specific effects. It has raised the profile of the issues associated with mental health and has challenged the views of those who have devalued the opinions of individuals who happen to have mental health problems. Involvement in a self-help or user group can serve as a support by being with people who may be coping with similar problems. It can also help to validate the perspectives of people who might not be being heard elsewhere and to problem-solve with respect to day-to-day issues of living.

Activism

The extent to which self-help groups are involved in activism varies. Some of the larger groups are linked with people in government and have a sufficiently high profile that their opinions on relevant issues receive national press attention. More locally based groups might have fewer connections of this type, but can still be highly effective in the local mental health and social care setting. It will be a matter for individual choice whether you feel that your needs are met through being involved in this way or whether your priorities are more towards the other services that might be available. Some people involved in this aspect of user groups have told us of the powerful benefits they have experienced for their own mental health. The act of being involved in trying to influence policy at a local health and national government level, although often frustrating, can reinforce the individual's sense of their own competence. One individual described being able to leave her symptoms to 'sort themselves out' during important meetings and that she would return to them later when it was more convenient for her. Clearly this increased sense of mastery over her own experiences was an important benefit from her active involvement in issues close to her heart.

Information

An important role for many of these organisations is that of providing information. People often lack information on the nature of their diagnosis and what it means, what treatment is being offered and why and what other options there might be for treatment or for other forms of support. There is also a great need for information on activities and employment and also on how legislation can be relevant to an individual seeking a return to the workplace or appropriate housing. If you have access to a computer, most of these organisations have their own websites. These usually provide helpful information on their publications and self-help materials. It can be informative to look at a number of these sites to see which publications might be most relevant to you at the present time. As you do this you will see that not all organisations agree or have the same perspective on all issues. Again it is useful to take a problem-solving approach to decide which approach is the most likely to be helpful for you.

 Jemma had managed to return to work as a librarian after a period of illness. She had been back at work for six months when her manager informed her that, due to re-organisation, her role would be changing. She had, until this point, worked mainly behind the scenes developing computerised index and search systems. This was an area that she was highly skilled at and from which she derived considerable satisfaction. It involved a lot of individual work on the computer, which Jemma preferred to having a lot of interpersonal contact. However, the role change would involve her spending a considerable amount of time dealing with the public, including providing regular tours of the library for new students. Jemma was ex-tremely distressed by this prospect. As she considered the possible impact of this change she felt increasingly under strain. She had never felt comfortable with working under the public gaze and was concerned that she would

Continued

become ill if forced to do so. Initially she did not know where to turn. However, she eventually discovered that a local user group provided support and information in relation to employment issues. She was also able to get useful information from her union representative. On the basis of this information she was able to meet with her manager to discuss her concerns and also her legal rights under current disability at work legislation. Her manager was sympathetic to Jemma's situation but felt that they would have to meet with his regional boss to sort the problem out. Jemma, having made contact with her local group was able to bring along an advocate to support her in this meeting. Jemma felt that this made the difference between her saying nothing and being able to present her case. Eventually it was agreed that it would fall within the legal requirement of 'reasonable adjustments' to permit Jemma to retain her old role. This was partly due to making the managers aware that this was a requirement of current legislation and partly because Jemma, with support, collected evidence of how her current role was valued by her peers. She also showed that her attendance record was in the top 10 per cent of her peers (which would have been at risk with the proposed change). Although Jemma found this a stressful experience, her achievement of the outcome she needed increased her confidence and actually led to her feeling more positive about staying in work.

Being heard by someone who has had similar experiences

In addition to any of the specific roles of user groups outlined above, there is also the key factor of having experiences heard by someone who understands through having had similar experiences. This can be facilitated through group work in professional settings, through informal friendship, or through self-help support groups. Many people who have had the experience of mental health problems feel that they are alone. This is because they may not knowingly have come into contact with anyone else with mental health problems prior to their own problems developing. Of course the chances are extremely high that they will have had prior contact with numerous people who have mental health problems without knowing it. Research figures indicate that mental health problems such as anxiety and depression of sufficient severity to merit psychiatric diagnosis are present in around twenty five per cent of the general population at any one time. Also, people will often regard their own symptoms or experiences as very different from those of others. Usually this is unhelpful, as it can be associated with seeing yourself as 'worse' than other people. This normally also means that it undermines a person's belief in their being able to live with the illness and problem-solve the difficulties associated with it.

Sharing these issues in a group setting can be very powerful, especially when it is a group that meets regularly so that people can get to know and understand each other's experiences well. A well-run group can be in any setting but must have ground rules concerning confidentiality and mutual respect. People are often astounded at the extent to which they share common experiences after attending a group of this type. In a safe setting people will often open up and describe experiences that, because they happen in your head, are private and often unknown to others. Without the benefit of this experience the feeling of loneliness can be compounded, because you can almost never tell from someone's behaviour precisely what inner experiences they are having.

Once you are aware that there is common ground with other people it then becomes possible to discuss coping approaches to common problems. This again can be very powerful, as in any group there will often be many years of experience of problem-solving with respect to symptom-related problems which each user can tap into. The groups will also perform an important validation function, as noted above – people often say that in this sort of setting they are able to recount experiences which they had previously rarely if ever discussed. Finally, finding that these events can be described to others and are not then reacted to as shameful or stupid or meaningless or weak is clearly empowering, as this is often a fear that people carry.

 Jim was wary about attending a hearing voices group. He had only told his partner and his psychiatrist about the voices he heard. He was ashamed that he still heard voices sometimes and thought that if anyone else knew they would reject him. This fear was partly triggered by the initial reactions of his work colleagues when he became ill for the first time. They had laughed at him when he asked if they were aware of people following him and had stopped inviting him out for a drink after work. At the first meeting with the group Jim was very quiet. He listened to other people in the group and was amazed. Several people recounted experiences very similar to his and all were heard with respect. He began to feel less afraid of discussing his own experiences. He worked up his courage over the following week and in the second group described some of his own experiences. People were interested in what he had to say and shared examples of when they had experienced similar reactions. This led to a problem-solving discussion about how to deal with the ignorance of some people and how to work out what to share with whom. Jim found this an extremely positive experience and began to use the group regularly to think through those of his experiences that he did not want to

Continued

discuss with his partner Rachel, for fear of her considering him ill. He felt that, as a result, pressures built up
less within him and his relationships with Rachel and his
family, over time, improved significantly.

Recovery models

Schizophrenia, or dementia praecox as it was first called, by Emil
Kraepelin in 1898, was seen as a disorder in which there is progressive deterioration of functioning and from which recovery
did not occur. This view has been influential in the field of psychiatry. Hence, for many people treatment has historically meant
taking medication to suppress symptoms as far as possible, with
very limited expectations of full recovery or even of recovery of
substantial areas of social and occupational functioning.

However, there is now substantial evidence that many
people with a diagnosis of schizophrenia can live productive
and full lives. The rates of people who experience recovery vary.
Initial psychiatric studies indicated ten to twenty per cent recovery, but more recent reports have been more optimistic; when
recovery is defined as the development of 'new meaning and
purpose as one grows beyond the catastrophe of mental illness'
(Anthony, 1993) several studies have estimated recovery rates
around fifty per cent or higher.

Although there are specific disputes about the extent to which
full remission of schizophrenic symptoms is possible, this can miss
the point of the recovery approach. Essentially the key message of
the recovery model is that the receipt of this diagnosis need not
imply that the person is doomed to be a passive recipient of anti-
psychotic medication and do nothing else of value for the rest of
their lives. Whether or not psychotic symptoms are experienced,
people can usually find ways to work around or with these symptoms to live full and productive lives. It might be that for some
people it is not possible to return to formal education and routine

office-based work. In the past this might have been taken as an indication that there is little left for the person to do. However this model emphasises that valued activities should be defined in a broader sense. Thus engagement in artistic activity, voluntary work in the church or charities or indeed within the self-help/ user movement is all of clear human value. Furthermore, with the development of computers the potential for individualised patterns of work and self-employment indicate possibilities to realise potential and employ skills without necessarily having to conform to standards that might impact negatively on mental health. It is worth noting here of course that disability discrimination legislation in both the UK and the US highlights the importance of firms making reasonable accommodation for people with disabilities, which includes those with mental health problems.

Informing the development of professional services

In the UK, most mental health and primary care trusts are required to have user representation. The involvement of user groups in academic establishments and in the training of mental health professionals is also increasing. This provides a relatively direct means by which the perspectives of users of mental health services can inform their further developments. Clearly, this does not mean that all user views can be accommodated and it is also likely that user representation will have different experiences in different areas, at least while this process is being established. However, the precedent is now firmly established that people who use mental health services have valuable experience and expertise to bring to bear on making these services helpful to the people who need them.

At an individual level this should also be reflected in people's attitude towards their own consumption of mental health services. In our view such services are most beneficial when user and provider work in collaboration. This means users taking an active role in their own treatment and having the courage to express their views. This is something that we actively encourage in our work, but we are also aware that it is not always easy. Usually it is possible to develop a mutually respectful relationship with your clinician and this is an important feature of successful therapy whether that is psychological or medical. Where this does not prove possible it may be necessary to identify whether there is another clinician available. If this is an issue there may be people within the mental health team who can help and again self-help groups may be a useful resource for information if required. It is usually the case that if you have access to a local mental health team who know you and with whom you are familiar, this can be beneficial.

Taking the best from both

There are limitations to mental health services and the individuals who work in them, and the same also applies to user groups. Equally, both have an important role to play in helping individuals to maximise their functioning and facilitate their progress towards important life goals. An active approach to living with a diagnosis of this type probably involves taking the best from both forms of support. The combination of features that make 'the best' will depend on your requirements as an individual. This will again be an issue where testing out possibilities within the services available might be helpful.

 Simon attended a part-time sheltered work scheme that he enjoyed and also went to meetings of his local user group that were independent of the hospital system. He also saw his psychiatrist once every three months and a care co-ordinator weekly. Over the years he discovered that he got different things from each of these resources.

Continued

He found his meetings with the psychiatrist valuable, but mostly focused on issues around medication. He talked more about day-to-day issues with his care co-ordinator and was also able to talk with her about issues such as possible medication changes or reductions, which he might be planning to raise at his next meeting with his psychiatrist. His meetings with the user group were helpful in keeping him informed about general issues concerning mental health and legislation. They were also where he felt most comfortable talking about his aims and goals for the future. There he felt he could get useful feedback on his ideas from people who might have tried similar things and he also felt that he could learn from the experiences of people who had had problems with achieving particular aims. His current issue was one of moving on from sheltered work into an open employment setting. This excited him, but he was also concerned about how he would cope with it. With the support of his fellow group members he found out information on transitional courses to help him move into open employment and eventually succeeded in doing this. He did find this stressful and there were times when he wondered if he had made the right choice. However, he did find over time that by discussing his concerns with his peers and also getting advice from his mental health workers, he coped. As he found he survived the ups and downs of his new role, his confidence increased and he became less anxious about brief increases in worrying thoughts or voices. He found that if he took prompt action to talk them through and also took time out to relax, these experiences normally passed without significant impact.

Points covered in this chapter

➡ Self-help fits well with a psychological approach to dealing with the problems associated with a diagnosis of schizophrenia. Both approaches agree on the importance of respecting the perspective of people who have life experience of dealing with schizophrenia.

➡ Self-help covers a broad range of activities, from information and general support to activism. People will vary on what aspects of these activities are most helpful for them.

➡ Self-help groups have increased in number and influence in recent years. The importance of the user movement is being acknowledged both in the UK and the US. UK legislation now formally requires user representation with respect to clinical services and clinical research.

➡ Advocacy counselling can be part of the self-help process. Advocacy help can come from self-help groups, it can also be provided through other voluntary organisations such as the Citizens Advice Bureau.

➡ Many self-help organisations offer counselling, which is valued by many users of services. There are also opportunities to try alternative medicine approaches both at self-help groups and through some mental health services.

➡ People often benefit from the support and validation that self-help groups can offer. The actual process of involvement in the activities of such groups can help to emphasise an individual's own coping skills and their valued role.

➡ Activism can also be an important role for self-help groups both locally and with respect to national policy issues.

➡ The provision of information is a key issue for many service users. Self-help groups often provide information services and publications that are relevant to dealing both with the psychological and practical aspects of living with a mental health problem.

➡ Being heard by others who have had similar experiences can have a very positive impact. This can challenge the sense of being alone and having problems that no one else might understand.

➡ Recovery models are increasingly showing that earlier views of schizophrenia were unduly pessimistic. They also highlight the importance of considering recovery within the context of an individual's life as a whole: rather than only with respect to the presence or absence of particular symptoms.

➡ User representatives are developing key roles in the implementation and development of mental health services. The mechanisms for this are still evolving, but such representation is likely to have an important impact on the way services are delivered in the future.

➡ Many people benefit from a combination of self-help and mental health service input, the amounts of each varying across individuals. It is often most useful to take a pragmatic approach, taking the best from both.

9

Work and practical issues (the importance of valued activities and goals)

Work

Work is often seen as being synonymous with paid employment. However, work is in fact any effortful activity in which a person engages to achieve a particular outcome. Thus the Merriam-Webster online dictionary defines work as:

> Activity in which one exerts strength or faculties to do or perform something: **a**: sustained physical or mental effort to overcome obstacles and achieve an objective or result **b**: the labor, task, or duty that is one's accustomed means of livelihood **c**: a specific task, duty, function, or assignment often being a part or phase of some larger activity.

This chapter is not about suggesting that all people should be in paid employment, or that only paid employment is of value. Rather, it is about the importance of having valued activities and goals.

Why activity is important

Activity is important because human beings, as with other animals, are naturally active. If we are deprived of purposeful activity we tend to react to this with irritability, frustration and lowering of mood. Purposeful activity is any activity that is aimed towards achieving a goal that is of value to the individual. There is much evidence from studies comparing people in and out of work that people who have become unemployed tend to suffer more physical and mental health problems than those who are in work. Although most studies have compared people in paid employment with those who are not, there is also research that suggests that regular work in unpaid activity has similar benefits. Additionally, some research with older adults is relevant here. Studies of individuals after retirement indicate that decline in cognitive and memory functioning is not an inevitable consequence of ageing. Rather, they show that people who continue to engage in activities that use cognitive and memory skills preserve their abilities in these areas to a large degree. This again suggests, for people in general, the importance of activities that stimulate cognitive and memory capabilities.

Activity naturally fluctuates during the day, usually peaking in the middle of the day and being less in mornings and evenings. This pattern is consistent with the internal time clock (or circadian rhythms) that we all have. This serves to keep us in tune with our external environment so that we are active during the day and usually able to sleep at night. Where we are inactive for long periods this can interfere with the functioning of the internal time clock and make it harder to sleep and harder to maintain activities.

Activity is also important in terms of mental well-being. Engaging in activity that is planned towards an outcome is generally rewarding. By doing things we discover both that we can do them and learn skills that help us to take on further challenges. We are exposed in doing this to both success and frustration. This can in itself be beneficial: through persisting we have the opportunity to discover that it is possible to cope with both.

Range of work possibilities

Full-time work

It is clear that not everyone who has a diagnosis of schizophrenia will be able to engage in full-time work. But, it is also equally important to be clear that this is a valid option for a proportion of people who have had this diagnosis. There are examples of people with this diagnosis who have worked in a wide range of jobs from the creative to the caring professions. Increasingly there is recognition of the importance of finding ways for people to return to work. Rufus May, a clinical psychologist, has made a powerful case for the importance of seeing the experience of schizophrenia from the perspective of those who have received the diagnosis. His voice is especially important as he was hospitalised with schizophrenia as an adolescent and yet managed subsequently to attend university and then qualify as a mental health professional. An extract written by Rufus May is printed below; it was originally published by the British Psychological Society in June 2000 ('Understanding mental illness: recent advances in understanding mental illness and psychotic experiences'):

> Starting employment doing work that was not too demanding was an important way for me to recover, starting off with part-time work a month or so after my third and final admission. The job was working in Highgate cemetery as a night security guard. I did once fall asleep on a late shift but my boss took an understanding approach and I held it down for the full nine months. I had a range of jobs, followed by four months doing voluntary care work with adults with learning disabilities. Being

trusted to carry out responsible and challenging work that I was valued for, was a real breakthrough and gave me the confidence to apply for paid work and make long-term plans to train as a clinical psychologist.

Obviously, while some people may feel driven to work within mental health, others will see this as an experience that is separate from their work interests. Thus people may be just as likely to find employment in libraries, garages or shops. Just as with anyone else, there are decisions to be made about what role is important to you as an individual. This will include an evaluation of the costs and benefits of potential jobs, including the balance between the stress associated with the role, compared with the positive benefits such as interest, salary, or other rewards. Equally, there are issues concerning what is possible for each person. Not everyone will be equipped to undertake university study and post-graduate education – irrespective of whether they happen to have a particular mental health diagnosis. Information from local employment services, mental health services and voluntary organisations can all be important in identifying what opportunities exist in your local area and how these fit with your talents and potential.

Part-time work

There is an increasing acceptance of the important role that part-time workers play in the economy. The advantage of this type of role is in the balance between stress and structure. There is a regular commitment, but you still have time to engage in other activities. Some people will use part-time work as a way of eventually getting into full-time employment. Other people will find that working in this way forms an appropriate balance for them. For instance, if being with people is stressful and difficult it may be that a job takes more out of you than it would under other circumstances. It may also be that not working at all, with its associated risk of social isolation, is also something to be avoided. In those circumstances, part-time work might be an appropriate option.

Jim had not worked for several years, since the onset of his illness. Prior to becoming unwell he had worked for his uncle's painting firm. Jim felt that he wanted to get back to work but was unsure that he could commit to full-time employment. After discussion with Rachel, his partner, he spoke with his uncle about the possibility of working for him part-time. He was also concerned about working for his uncle, as some of the people who had worked there when he had become unwell had had a very negative attitude towards him. As he had been a good worker in the past, his uncle agreed to take him on again as a painter and decorator, on a part-time basis. It was initially agreed that he would take jobs where he worked alone, as he built up his confidence. After several months he felt able to work on larger projects with other employees. To his relief the people with whom he had had problems had moved on. He was able to get on with his new work colleagues and was pleased to find that he could still perform well at his job. He did find both the work and social contact tiring and has decided to date that the right balance for him is to work two to three days per week.

Casual or temporary work

Another approach that some people take is to take work more informally. Work is seen as something that can be helpful, but there is recognition that it is not appropriate all the time. This can again be when someone is recovering from an illness episode or exploring whether a change in his or her routine is sustainable. Setting this up so that there is an end in sight through temporary work can seem less daunting than committing to the demands of a permanent contract. Obviously, the downside to this in the longer term is that such posts are by their nature temporary and their financial rewards unpredictable. They also involve contact with different and unfamiliar groups of people, which can be a source of strain in its own right for some individuals.

> Sam had learnt a range of office skills through a number of courses that she had undertaken at her local college. She wanted to find work to use these skills, but she was worried about committing herself to this. Initially she felt that she would not be able to use her skills, but then discussed this with her friends and with people at her local support group. She then decided to talk with a number of temporary employment agencies about providing clerical services on a temporary basis. Although she found the contact with new people quite stressful, she enjoyed knowing that each task would only last up to a couple of months. After several such contracts she found that her confidence increased. Sam began to be less concerned that her mental health problems would undermine her work performance. She also began to notice that her mood fluctuations seemed less severe when she was engaged in tasks that felt constructive. At this time she was just beginning to consider the possibility of moving from temporary contracts to take up a permanent offer from a local firm for whom she had recently worked.

Supported employment

Local organisations, such as those included in the Association for Supported Employment in the UK (contact details provided in Appendix 1), work with a range of people, including people with mental health problems. Such organisations within this association generally look to match the individual's needs and talents with appropriate work opportunities. This type of service can provide an important link into the employment market for people who have not been in employment for some time. There is also an increasing awareness of the need for flexibility rather than a 'one size fits all' approach. Thus, whereas qualities in one setting may be regarded as unhelpful, in another setting they may be extremely appropriate. A person who finds lots of social contact difficult may thrive in an environment that a more extrovert person might find isolating. Neither reaction is right or wrong; it is just different. Thus, the example in chapter 8 concerning Jemma was that she thrived in an environment that required that she often work alone, but when faced with the possibility of a role change that might include a lot of contact with the public became very concerned. Hence, it is helpful when there are resources to match people to jobs and to work actively to develop opportunities for people with additional needs. This approach is actively supported by the British Government (Department for Work and Pensions) whose own role through Job Centre Plus is to facilitate access to employment for people with additional needs, including providing additional resources to help people to do appropriate jobs (for US equivalents contact your State Labor Office; contact information is in Appendix 1). Those areas that have a Job Centre Plus offer personal advisers to help individuals work their way through the complications of finding appropriate employment in the context of their other needs. There are currently approximately 140 of these centres across the UK at present, with targets for coverage of all UK towns by 2006.

Voluntary work

This is another important area and has been used by many people as either an alternative to paid employment or as a means to gaining confidence to re-enter the workplace. There are many roles possible here. These can range from giving some time to a local charity shop, to becoming involved in work to protect wildlife or restore important community facilities. This is an important area of work for a wide range of people from adolescents to those of retirement age. Some people engage in this in addition to their main work in order to 'give something back' and often to obtain job satisfaction, which might be missing from their particular paid employment. Alternatively, other people may work almost full time in a voluntary role dedicated to an issue about which they care passionately. There are numerous sources of information about possibilities which exist in this area (also listed with full contact details in Appendix 1), which include:

1. Do It Yourself. This is a web service based in America. It recognises that for many reasons, people do not always wish to commit large amounts of time or to volunteer through large organisations. This Charity Guide website provides information on many aspects of volunteering, including ways of making a difference independently, or through using a home computer.

2. National Association for Volunteer Bureaux. Volunteer Bureaux are recruitment and advice centres for potential volunteers across the UK. They can provide information to help you decide what type of voluntary work is available locally and what would be most appropriate for your skills and interests. Volunteer Bureaux can also be listed as Volunteer Centres, Councils for Voluntary Service, Voluntary Action or Volunteer Development Agencies.

3. Timebank. The idea for this web-based service came from the founders of Comic Relief. The campaign encourages people to give as much or as little time as they choose. The website provides information on a wide range of volunteering opportunities across the UK.

There will be many other ways of finding out about volunteering in your local area. Information of this type is often posted in local libraries, GP surgeries and local authority buildings. There are also often advertisements in the local press and information available through other local people who may be able to feedback their own experience of volunteering.

> Simon had always been interested in animals. He did think about whether he might find a job working with animals, but was unsure whether he could cope with this at the time. He was talking to a friend who also had mental health problems, who suggested that he look into voluntary work first. To begin with Simon was unsure as how to proceed. After discussing this with his parents and his support group, he got a number of ideas. Eventually he found a local dog rescue centre which was asking for volunteers to help on a regular basis. Simon visited the centre and thought that the work they wanted him to do would be manageable. He started volunteering for a day each week and eventually built this up to two and a half days, which he feels very positive about.

Doing something of interest

Although there are many organisations which are set up to provide help and support in voluntary and paid employment, it is important not to lose sight of the initial quote at the beginning of this chapter. Working includes anything that requires the use of effort or skills employed towards to an important outcome. This includes deciding for your own reasons for instance that you wish to learn to use a computer, paint a picture or learn a language. These activities are valuable to the extent that they help you to achieve important personally valued goals. We should not assume that appropriate work is only work if defined as such by other organisations. Making decisions about what your areas of interest are and how to pursue them constructively is crucial. Often this process is made easier by discussing ideas with friends, family or people you trust within your self-help or professional support network. It is often useful to start off with as broad a range of ideas as possible and then refine these down as you think in more detail about each possible option. Deciding on this is important, whether you think that you can eventually work in this area as a full-time paid employee or whether it is an interest to be explored on a part-time or casual basis.

Barriers to employment

There are a number of possible barriers to employment that, in our experience, people with a diagnosis of schizophrenia have identified. These are considered below, in turn.

Lack of confidence

It is understandable that if you have not been in the workplace for some time then it may be difficult to feel confident in applying for work. The approach of this book is generally a problem-solving one. In this situation the first step would be to identify what it might be possible to do without undue distress. This might in the first instance be looking through a local paper, talking to friends and family or discussing the initial thoughts with a professional. It would be important to give yourself permission to take your time and to realise that a decision to seek out information does not commit you to the next steps of seeking work, unless you choose to do this. Confidence issues may also be to do with the mental health problems that you are experiencing. This might be a useful target of therapy if you are seeing a psychologist or other mental health professional for psychological treatment. Also, beginning to explore possible activities in general can be helpful both in building up confidence and also in clarifying what sorts of environments are likely to suit you.

Lack of ideas

Again, if it is a while since you have concentrated your thoughts on this issue, you might find at first that you feel a little rusty. It might be hard to think of things that you might want to pursue and how you might want to do it. Ideas can come from anywhere, from discussions with friends or family for instance, from reading or from surfing the web. One thing that people tend to do when they are trying to think around this issue is to 'edit' their thinking too early. That is, as soon as an idea begins to form it is rejected because 'it's too difficult', 'it's not possible', 'that will never happen', or 'it's not worth the effort'. In general problem-solving, as well as in this particular situation, it can be very helpful to brainstorm ideas. This normally involves writing down any ideas that occur and consciously deciding not to edit them (at least not at first). To aid this process, it can often be helpful to include items that you think are silly or impossible. Thus it is most unlikely that many of us will become astronauts or belly dancers, but if it occurs to you then put it down. Once you have a list you can then begin to think, for each idea, what it is you need to find out to decide whether it is one you wish to pursue. Through this process it can quite quickly be possible to generate two or three possibilities for further detailed investigation.

If you are struggling to get started, here is a list of thirty-three possibilities from which you might want to select to 'kick-start' your brainstorming. These are just ideas generated at random, so feel free to include or reject any of these according to your interests and skills. Be sure to add your own particular ideas once you have got started with generating ideas, as your own ideas will generally be the best ones.

BRAINSTORM LIST

Student, lawyer, bus driver, shop assistant, librarian, bricklayer, computer programmer, clerical assistant, secretary, warehouse person, van driver, factory worker, lorry driver, traffic warden, park keeper, counsellor, staff or volunteer trainer, web designer, artist, musician, plasterer, home-worker, social worker, nurse, psychologist, historian, electrician, plumber, painter and decorator, writer, security guard.

Lack of support

People often feel isolated and unsupported. There are a number of organisations, which are listed in Appendix 1, that are there to help with this issue. Although it may feel difficult to get in touch with them in the first instance, once this has been done they can normally provide information and support. This will often also involve contact with other people in similar circumstances going through the same processes. In addition to formal organisations it is also important not to forget to draw on the help of any informal networks of friends or relatives that you have. Most people have experience of work of some type and may be sources of information or support. Obviously, with both formal and informal sources of support it is important to use your own judgement to assess whether the information given to you is helpful and relevant to the problem that you are trying to resolve.

Fear or ignorance of others

As noted elsewhere in this book, people have differing views regarding mental illness. It is unfortunately still the case that some people have very negative views of people with a history of mental health problems. This is a situation that has often not been helped by the stereotypes portrayed in the national press. It is understandable that there can sometimes be reluctance among people with a diagnosis of schizophrenia to put themselves into public situations, such as a work environment. It is also important to note that both the user movement and professional groups have been working to reduce public ignorance about mental health issues with some success. The more people who are able to enter the workplace with a mental health history and demonstrate their contribution, the harder it will be for the minority of people with strong negative views to sustain them. It is also worth repeating that population surveys indicate high rates of anxiety and depression in the general population, so people with a mental health history are actually already commonplace in working environments.

Legislation

In the UK since 1996 it has been illegal for employers of more than fifteen people to discriminate against people with disabilities. They are breaking the law if they treat an employee or job applicant less favourably, or do not make reasonable adjustments to accommodate someone with a disability. Although the legislation appears to be written primarily with people with physical disabilities in mind it does also cover people with mental health problems. This means that there is official government recognition of the importance of finding employment for people who historically may not have been given the chance to demonstrate their talents due to a history of either physical or mental health problems. This does not mean that all employers will act in a reasonable manner, but it does mean that employees have the law on their side if they are treated unreasonably because of a mental health problem. It also means that other services, such as supported employment agencies, who are aware of this legislation, can use it as one of the bases for negotiation with a wide range of potential employers. This legislation was referred to in chapter 8 when Jemma needed to negotiate with her managers concerning what it was reasonable to ask her to do.

Support in finding activities

The information provided in this volume is not intended to be a complete guide, but rather to point people in the right direction so that they can obtain information specific to their particular needs. It is likely that many people will find it helpful to obtain support in the challenging process of identifying work that is right for them. There are numerous resources to help with this, which include:

Government employment service

The *Job Centre Plus* programme (see Appendix 1) is intended to help people into employment and training. This includes the *Access to Work* scheme, which provides information, advice and funding to employers to address any additional cost of employing a disabled person. *New deal* provides job brokers and aims to support job seekers through liaison with employers and to provide help with presentational skills including preparation of curricula vitae. *Job introduction scheme* provides grants to employers if they or the employee are concerned that a disability may interfere with their ability to do the job. *Work preparation courses* orient people to the skills and demands associated with returning to or starting out in a working environment.

Self-help groups

There are many local and national self-help groups, including MIND, Making Space and Hearing Voices Network in the UK, and the National Alliance for the Mentally Ill and Schizophrenics Anonymous in the US (see Appendix 1 for details). These are all important sources of information for people with a diagnosis of schizophrenia. They can often provide helpful information and advice on work-related issues. The larger self-help groups can also provide employment and voluntary opportunities. In addition, it can be helpful to find out from fellow consumers of mental health services how they have addressed the problem of work. An example in the Hearing Voices Network and elsewhere has been the development of training packs by service users which have become independent businesses providing information on mental health issues from a user perspective to professional and voluntary agencies.

Occupational therapy departments

Most mental health services have within them an occupational therapy department. Part of the role of this department will normally be to provide activities for people who might either be in hospital or require additional support. They will also often be a very valuable source of information about employment, education and training in your local area. Many occupational therapists will have been involved in developing programmes specifically designed to meet the needs of people with mental health problems wishing to return to some form of work or training.

Money

Managing money is an issue for all of us. The amount of money we have and the source of that income are important in deciding what might be realistic work choices for us, as well as affecting other important aspects of our lives. Many people who have a diagnosis of schizophrenia will receive state benefits of one form or another. In the UK such benefits might include incapacity benefit, severe disablement allowance (which is being withdrawn), disability living allowance and housing benefit. The rules of entitlement and the precise range of benefits vary and it is often difficult to ensure that you are receiving all the benefit that you are entitled to. One source of information and advice can be through your mental health team, who are often able to help with this. In addition, Disability Centres in the UK (part of the Department for Work and Pensions) can provide information as can many self-help organisations and the Citizens Advice Bureau. Taking an active role to ensure that you receive the funds to which you are entitled is important. This is also key when checking how taking up different types of employment might affect any benefits that you do receive.

Another issue is that of debt. Many people with a diagnosis of schizophrenia can have debt problems associated with periods of illness. Rent, loans or other payments may not have been kept up during periods of ill-health. If debts have increased in this way it can be tempting to ignore them and get on with other things. This is understandable and many people have this reaction, irrespective of whether they have a mental health problem or not. However, this will cause you greater problems in the long run and as bills escalate and contact from lenders gets more threatening, the distress associated with this situation is often made worse. Again, it can be important to get help, in these situations, to negotiate with lenders. The mental health team are often involved in helping people negotiate with lenders; help is, as above, also available from a number of voluntary organisations, such as the Citizens Advice Bureau. In the US, non-profit debt assistance is available from agencies including Ameridebt and Profina Debt Solutions. This help will usually enable an agreement to be reached on a debt repayment plan. Acting early, in getting advice as soon as you are aware of a problem, is the best policy here.

Housing

As noted in chapter 2, historically there used to be a view that a diagnosis of schizophrenia was associated with inevitable chronic illness and decline. For many years the majority of people with schizophrenia were thought to require long-term hospital care. This situation has changed now and the vast majority of people with a diagnosis of schizophrenia live in the general community. Finding the right balance between independence and support can be very important in maintaining your mental health at the best level possible. For some people that will mean living entirely alone with no formal support, for others differing levels of support with accommodation might be appropriate.

Supported accommodation

This varies from hostels that are permanently staffed, to flats that have regular visits from support workers. These forms of accommodation are often accessed through the local authority or mental health services referral. Information and advice can usefully be obtained through your mental health team or local self-help groups. In the US there are state and federal schemes providing supported housing for people with mental health problems. Again, information on provision in a particular state is usually best obtained through local community health centres or the state government's department of human services.

Simon had struggled with living with his parents. As indicated in chapter 10, it was eventually decided that there might be less tension between them if Simon lived elsewhere. Initially Simon rented a small flat across town from his parents. He liked the independence that this gave him, but he struggled with shopping, cleaning and paying bills in addition to his other activities. He discussed this with his care co-ordinator as he was concerned that the pressure might lead to him becoming unwell again. After a couple of months his care co-ordinator was able to find him a flat in a supported housing scheme nearby. This compromise has worked well for Simon. He still has a substantial amount of independence, but he also has access to help and support, as he needs it, from the support workers attached to the project.

Respite accommodation

It is recognised that some people generally cope well either living alone or with their families. There may be periods when due to poorer mental health or because of other difficulties, time-limited periods of additional support would be helpful. In recognition of this, respite hostels have been set up to provide support when it is needed but with flexibility for the person to return to more independent living when this is no longer required. Again local information is often best accessed through mental health services, local authorities, or self-help groups.

Support for independent living

For some people with a diagnosis of schizophrenia, it may be difficult to access support networks that many of us rely on. If there have been periods of hospitalisation together with family relationship difficulties, it can be problematic to make a life alone without support. Self-help groups and local authorities can provide information on this important issue. There is now much more of an awareness of how sensible it is to provide people with the flexible support they need to live independently, rather than assuming that anyone who struggles to cope entirely on their own is therefore in need of long-term supported housing.

Points covered in this chapter

➡ Work is not just paid employment, it is any effortful activity directed towards a particular outcome.

➡ Regular activity is important for everyone. Having access to regular purposeful activity is associated with health and mood benefits for everyone, including people with a diagnosis of schizophrenia.

➡ There are many different types of paid employment. It is important to evaluate what sort of employment is most appropriate for you. This will vary, depending on the extent of your emotional difficulties.

➡ Full-time employment is a realistic option for some people with a diagnosis of schizophrenia.

➡ Part-time employment is often a helpful way into the employment market, or may be a good long-term option for some people.

➡ Casual/temporary work is sometimes useful for people who do not feel able to commit to long periods of sustained work.

➡ Supported employment is another important option that is facilitated by local agencies and has government backing.

➡ People often find that suitable forms of employment may vary over time depending on individual health and also opportunities available.

➡ There are many opportunities for voluntary work. There are a number of national organisations that provide information on this. It is also worth investigating local opportunities in your own area.

➡ Doing something of interest is also a purposeful activity. If formal work or volunteering does not appeal, then music, poetry, painting or learning are all valuable purposeful activities.

➡ Seeking support and taking a step-by-step approach can help to increase confidence in relation to employment issues.

➡ Ideas about what work might be suitable can be stimulated by discussing with others and by brainstorming possibilities.

➡ Appendix 1 lists a range of voluntary and government organisations that support people with mental health problems in the search for work.

➤ Legislation is now intended more actively to support people with mental health problems who wish
to work.

➤ Government job centres, self-help groups and occupational therapy departments can often be valuable
sources of information and support in identifying
activities.

➤ Managing money can be difficult, especially if you
do not receive all the benefits to which you are entitled. Mental health teams and self-help groups can
provide information to ensure you receive the money
that is rightfully yours.

➤ Debt is an issue for many people. You should not
ignore this and hope it will go away. Often, with help
from the Citizens Advice Bureau or care co-ordinators
debt problems can be resolved so that they do not
become a major source of strain.

➤ Housing alternatives are important. Most people want
to live as independently as possible, but might require
some support. Alternatives can include supported accommodation, respite accommodation and support with independent living.

10

The role of the family

Background information

Modern society has been characterised as synonymous with 'the breakdown of the family'. Very probably, more people live alone today than at any other time in history. However, for many people the family remains very important. People live with a range of family members, from parents to partners to children, and many others remain in contact with other members of their family. Further, it is very unlikely that any serious misfortune can affect someone without it affecting other members of their family. This is certainly true of serious illnesses, such as cancer or diabetes, and it is also true of many other problems: drug abuse, a serious accident, or problems with people outside the family, such as unemployment or debt. By the same token, when a family member has the kind of problems that lead to a diagnosis of schizophrenia, others in the family are bound to be affected. A considerable amount of research has now been done on the family 'burden' in schizophrenia. This research indicates the extent to which family members experience difficulties associated with supporting someone who has a diagnosis of schizophrenia. Research has also shown that families can have a big impact on the health and functioning of sufferers. This chapter will discuss both of these issues, and also look at some of the forms of help and support available to families.

In this section, one point needs to be emphasised; the discussion that follows is not meant to suggest that families are to blame for the symptoms that the person with a diagnosis of schizophrenia is experiencing. In the past, as explained in chapter 4, some thinkers suggested that schizophrenic illnesses could be blamed either on distant, unloving mothers or on families that had distorted patterns of communication. These theories had some following until the middle of the twentieth century, but recent research has shown no evidence to support them. This is not to say that unloving parents or other family problems have no effect; evidence has linked family history with a number of psychological and psychiatric problems, but not specifically with schizophrenia. However, families are sometimes reluctant to seek help for a member with some form of serious mental illness because they worry that they will be blamed. There is no point in blaming either sufferers or their families; blame achieves nothing, while, in contrast, practical action can achieve a lot to help both sufferers and their families to cope better.

Stresses in the family

As noted above, a great deal of research has now been done on the effects of schizophrenia on family life. Two points emerge very clearly: that having a family member who suffers from schizophrenia can place great stress on other family members, and that some families can also cause stress to sufferers by the ways that they react. The result can be a vicious cycle; as noted in chapter 7, stress can make symptoms of psychosis worse.

Thus, if a sufferer has the sorts of problems described earlier in this book, and the family reacts with anger or excessive criticism, the problems or symptoms can become worse. As will be discussed below, excessive stress can precipitate large increases in symptoms, sometimes resulting in hospitalisation, and this can make the whole family situation worse.

After Simon's first illness, he came back to live with his parents, but all of them found this very difficult. Simon's parents had taken great pride in his academic accomplishments, explained proudly to their neighbours that he was doing very well and had a wonderful career ahead of him. When Simon first became ill his parents responded in different ways. His mother lavished a lot of care and attention on him, worrying about his eating and sleeping and constantly asking him about how he was feeling. His father criticised him, saying that he needed to study more and that 'good things need to be worked for'. Simon took to avoiding his parents, sleeping late to avoid them in the morning and staying up to watch television after they had gone to bed, but he still found both his mother's worrying and his father's criticisms very stressful.

Simon's parents showed two very common types of family reaction to the sorts of symptoms and behaviours that are often associated with the diagnosis of schizophrenia. His mother, in her natural concern, showed *over-involvement*; she had a desire to protect and care for Simon but carried it too far. His father, not understanding what was happening to Simon, chose to show his concern through *criticism*; he hoped that in this way he could motivate Simon to return to his studies. Unfortunately, however well-meaning, these responses are often unhelpful, as we will see below.

Research suggests that two types of behaviour can be especially stressful for family members: bizarre behaviour and negative symptoms. As explained throughout this book, sufferers may have experiences, such as having unusual beliefs or hearing voices, which cause them to behave in unusual ways. These ways make perfect sense to them, but often seem odd and incomprehensible to strangers. Family members can be caught in the middle, wanting to support their loved one but also feeling uncomfortable or embarrassed at the reactions of others. They may try to control their loved one's behaviour by either being extra supportive, by criticising odd behaviour in the hope of suppressing it, or by 'walking on eggshells', that is, being extra careful not to upset or contradict the sufferer.

> When Jim first became ill, Rachel, his girlfriend, found it very frightening. When he talked oddly or voiced strange opinions, she was afraid to contradict him, and so would agree with everything that he said. Since she had previously been a person who wasn't afraid to voice her own opinions, Jim noticed this and found it strange; in fact, at times it would annoy him. In the end Rachel found a better way to deal with Jim; she would tell him when she disagreed with him, but would avoid arguing with him, since she knew that he believed very firmly in what he was saying. She also learnt through trial and error how to encourage him to take care of himself, without nagging and antagonising him.

So-called 'negative symptoms' explained in chapter 3 (pp. 26–28), can also be very difficult for families and loved ones. People who develop such symptoms can be very socially withdrawn and seem unmotivated, finding it very hard to do anything. Sometimes their self-care can be badly affected, and they may become solitary and avoid dealing with other people. Sometimes family members may attribute this to 'laziness', as Simon's father did, but this is not helpful. Current thinking suggests that social withdrawal and lack of activity may actually be helpful, in that they reduce stress. However, there is a balance to be achieved here, as too much withdrawal and lack of activity is also associated with low mood and depression. Criticism and over-involvement are each, in their own way, stressful, and they may actually make negative symptoms and their effects worse. So is there another possible response?

Family responses: Is there a better way?

As noted in the previous sections, over-involvement and criticism represent common ways in which families deal with difficult behaviours. This pattern can be observed with a variety of symptoms and problems, ranging from asthma to weight loss. However, when dealing with the types of problems often grouped under the label of schizophrenia, such responses can be unhelpful. In fact, research conducted over the last forty years suggests that a family environment with high levels of over-involvement and criticism can lead to increased stress, increased levels of symptoms, and the increased likelihood of a hospital admission. Over-involvement and criticism are often referred to together by the term 'expressed emotion', and families high in expressed emotion have been shown to have adverse effects on sufferers. By the same token, there are families that have also been shown to be low in expressed emotion. In such families, members seem to be calmer and more matter of fact, and to try as much as possible to handle difficulties as they arise. For example, in the previous vignette Rachel learnt through trial and error that certain approaches worked better with Jim than others did.

Over the years, both Simon and his parents have made great progress in learning to get along. One important step was that his parents accepted that Simon might be better off if he didn't live with them. This was especially difficult for this mother to accept, because she felt guilty about not being there for Simon at all times, but she gradually came to realise that the new arrangement was better for the whole family. Simon's parents also learnt to focus on issues that were most important to them, such as how Simon behaves in their company or when visiting their house. In many other areas of Simon's life they have come to realise that they must leave him to work things out for himself. This does not mean that things are always harmonious between them, but it does mean that on the whole they get on much better.

Three points are important. First, as noted above, blame and criticism should be avoided; neither the sufferer nor his or her family is to blame for the problems that they are trying to deal with. Whatever one thinks about the idea of schizophrenia as an illness, it can be helpful to think of it as some sort of medical process with biological roots, like diabetes or asthma. These are not the sufferer's fault, but they can be managed in helpful or unhelpful ways by sufferer and family. Second, a calm focus on solving immediate problems is usually helpful. If the sufferer appears unmotivated and uninterested in things, small steps and the establishment of reasonable routines are probably the most productive way to proceed. Finally, both sufferer and family need space and privacy. Being excessively intrusive and trying to manage your loved one's life will probably only lead to conflicts. Family members also need space to live their own lives; caregivers who take time for fulfilling activities are not uncaring but trying to look after themselves, and this is good for everyone in the family.

Of course all this is easier said than done. It is often hard for people to behave in a calm and rational manner precisely because of their love of and sense of responsibility for their loved one. Problems are especially likely to arise when, as in Simon's case, the sufferer's problems developed in late adolescence and early adulthood. This can be a difficult time in any case, and parents often feel they have the responsibility to intervene in their children's lives, irrespective of the nature or degree of their problems. Remember, however, that trying to lower one's expressed emotion is not the same as not caring; often keeping a cool head and maintaining a certain distance can make the help that one does give more effective.

Help for families

As noted above, research has increasingly shown that families can have a strong influence on the health and functioning of those who suffer from the types of symptoms and difficulties described throughout this book. This fact has led to greater knowledge about the kinds of help and support that families need to cope. Unfortunately, greater knowledge does not always translate into greater availability; specialist services for families can be thin on the ground and overstretched. However, help is slowly becoming more available.

This help can come in two forms. First, mental health professionals are increasingly being encouraged to take families into account, to consult with them, and to offer them information and support. If a member of your family has been diagnosed with a serious mental illness, you have the right to consult with members of the treatment team dealing with that person. Of course there are exceptions to this, especially if the family member in question does not want you to be involved. In general, laws about confidentiality give patients the right to keep details of their treatment private. If your relative so chooses, he or she can forbid the treating team to release any details to the family. However, if your relative agrees, you have the right to be privy to decisions regarding care and treatment and to make your opinions and wishes known. As discussed below, mental health laws in many countries and across the United States give special rights to a person's Next of Kin or Nearest Living Relative and that person may need to be consulted about matters such as involuntary detention or enforced medication. Services are also being developed to support families and caregivers, and these services may offer information about symptoms and treatment as well as help and advice. Support groups are also being established for caregivers, so that people with similar problems can meet to talk both about the stress involved in caring and about practical ways of coping. These would seem to be eminently sensible and cost-effective procedures, since in this as in so many cases, families do much of the work of caring that would otherwise have to be done by professionals.

A more specific form of family help is now also becoming available. 'Family therapy' is the term for types of psychological interventions aimed at families, with the intention of helping the family cope with the specific problems of one member. There are many types of family therapy and many different schools and theories as to how it might be done. However, in the last forty years or so specific family therapy interventions have been devised to help families in which one member suffers from schizophrenia. This type of therapy is based on the research discussed previously. Its main aim is to reduce expressed emotion in families and to help family members use the kind of calm, problem-solving, non-blaming approach discussed in the previous section. Treatment sessions will generally involve members of the family, including the sufferer, meeting with one or two therapists on a regular basis. Family members will be provided with information about how to manage their problems and will also be taught to relate together in new ways. This may take place in the session, and the sufferer and family members may also be given tasks to carry out between sessions.

Research trials have been done on family therapy for families high in conflict and expressed emotion, and the results have been encouraging. The therapy has been shown to help families reduce criticism and over-involvement and this has been shown to translate into better functioning for all family members and a lower rate of relapse for the diagnosed family member. Training in the principles of this approach is gradually being disseminated, and if you think it might be helpful, it is certainly worth finding out if something of this sort is available in your area.

As noted above, Simon and his family profited a great deal from a period of family therapy. Simon's parents felt very responsible for him and this led to them behaving intrusively. The therapist helped them to see that taking a more 'laid back' approach did not make them bad parents and in fact was better for Simon and better for them as well. They have also learnt that they get on better with him if they avoid the tendency to phone him up too often. The therapist helped them to see that they could maintain regular contact with Simon without having to feel that they must always know where he was and what he was doing. Simon also learnt how to handle his parents more effectively. He used to argue with them, whereas now he is generally able to listen to their advice, thank them for it, and then make his own decisions about what he wants to do. Another very important intervention by the therapist was to persuade Simon's parents to join a lawn bowling club. Worrying and trying to care for Simon had left his mother and father very isolated. Getting involved with the bowling club made

Continued

> them much less socially isolated and gave them more so-
> cial support; this made them feel better and also helped
> them to cope more effectively with their anxiety about
> Simon.

Families and the law

If a member of your family has been diagnosed with a serious mental illness, you may wish to enquire about various
legal aspects of this fact. As noted above, in most countries
and states the Nearest Living Relative or Next of Kin has considerable importance in terms of mental health law. Doctors
may be obliged to consult with that person about various care
issues, and in some cases that person will have considerable say
in treatment decisions. If a specific law is being applied to a
sufferer, perhaps to detain that person or administer involuntary
treatment, the Next of Kin may well need to be informed, and
in fact supplied with a considerable amount of information. In
some cases, patients and their families may receive legal advice,
or even the services of a lawyer, to help with these decisions. If
you are in this situation, it is certainly worthwhile informing
yourself of your legal rights and responsibilities.

Another problem may arise if a family member sufferers from
periods of illness and incapacity and is unable to take decisions
about matters such as finance. If the family member is agreeable,
a Power of Attorney can easily be set up allowing some other
designated individual to take legal decisions for the sufferer. In
this case, the sufferer is generally able to revoke that Power of
Attorney and resume complete control of his or her affairs at
any time. However, there is also a procedure that allows family
members to take permanent control of a member's affairs, obviously a much more serious legal step. This has different names
in different places; in the UK it is called Applying to the Court of
Protection. This procedure generally calls for medical evidence,

a legal decision, and various safeguards to make sure that the person taking over the control of another person's affairs is carrying out his or her duty in a conscientious manner. It is clearly a very serious step, and the sufferer has the legal right to contest it. It could also be a very painful step, since it implies the belief that a family member is permanently incapable of managing his or her affairs. We would not recommend it except in extreme cases, but if you do feel it is necessary, the obvious first step would be to consult a lawyer.

Points covered in this chapter

➡ Families play an important role in caring for many people who suffer from the symptoms of schizophrenia. Such caring can place great burdens on families.

➡ Living with a diagnosis of schizophrenia is difficult for the individual and for those around him or her. Emotional over-involvement and hostile criticism are common reactions to the behaviour of sufferers, but these reactions can be unhelpful.

➡ Two common causes of stress within families are odd and embarrassing behaviours and negative symptoms, that is, withdrawal and apathy.

➡ These symptoms are best approached with a calm, problem-solving approach that avoids blame and criticism.

➡ It is best to focus on a few achievable tasks and set firm but reasonable limits. These tasks and limits will be most effective if they are identified through discussion and mutual agreement.

➡ All members of a family need privacy and time to enjoy themselves, rather than feeling that they must focus on the problems of one family member. Having

time to yourself and interests of your own is important for anyone and helps in dealing with stressful
situations.

➡ Professional help is increasingly becoming available
to help families with problems of this nature.

11

Living with it

Introduction

As we hope we have made clear, we intend this book to be useful to people with a wide variety of experiences and problems. Although we assume that the majority of our readers have probably been given a diagnosis of schizophrenia, we certainly do not assume that all of them have accepted this as the description of their problem. Some readers may well doubt the meaning of the diagnosis or believe that their problems have another source altogether. We have also tried to make clear that the kinds of experiences and problems discussed in this book may or may not be long-lasting, and we certainly believe that recovery is a reasonable goal for most sufferers. However, if you have read this far, it is likely that your problems and difficulties are fairly severe, and also that they have proved to be long-lasting. So in this final chapter we try to look at some possible long-term problems and in what ways they might be addressed.

Stigma and discrimination

It is an unfortunate fact that people diagnosed with a variety of mental illnesses often suffer from fear and misunderstanding on the part of members of the public. Unfortunately, research shows that ordinary people are not well-informed about the causes and symptoms of mental illnesses, and that many people find the thought of mental illness frightening and disturbing. This fear is often not helped by the media, in which stories about mentally ill people committing bizarre crimes sometimes feature. It is also not helped by thoughtless use of language: some people use terms like 'crazy' or 'a nutter' as the ultimate form of insult. Of course this view is not universal: surveys also show that many people do understand the effects of mental illness and that greater knowledge can help people to become more compassionate. But the existence of these prejudiced views can have a number of bad effects.

For one thing, the existence of such prejudices can make people very reluctant to seek treatment or help for psychological or psychiatric problems. This can apply to a variety of problems ranging from schizophrenia to phobias and depression. People often associate the label of mental illness with seeking psychiatric treatment, so naturally sufferers may deny their need for help. As we discussed in chapter 4, the term 'schizophrenia' is associated with a number of specific, stigmatising beliefs. As we tried to show, these beliefs have little basis in fact and do a great deal of harm. Unfortunately, it is hard to change public opinion; those who are the most uninformed are often those who are least interested in learning about the subject. That being so, if you feel that you are suffering from prejudice and discrimination, what can you do about it?

First, if possible, you should avoid self-blame. Whatever your view of your problems, you did not choose to bring them on yourself. Many scientists believe that mental illnesses have both physical and psychological causes, causes in the brain and body. Like diabetes and asthma, they are conditions that cause difficulty and distress, and feelings of shame and self-blame can only make that worse.

'But a mental illness diagnosis leads to so much fear and mistrust. How can I live with that?' This is a good question. Neither of us has been diagnosed with a major mental illness, so it is probably much easier for us to offer wise advice than for many of our readers to put it into practice. The best advice we can offer is to try to remember that people expressing ignorant or prejudiced views are revealing much more about themselves than about the people they are talking about. Many groups of people have faced discrimination and overcome it. If you face discrimination, the best strategy is to respond calmly and assertively, and to try to remember that your value as a human being is not decreased by a label that has been put on you. As discussed earlier in this book, the user movement is also important in both providing support for individuals and in working to raise the profile and reduce the stigma attached to mental health issues.

One situation that sometimes arises can present a special problem. Suppose someone makes a joke or comment in your presence, unaware that you have received a mental illness diagnosis. Should you speak out and try to show that person that they are in the wrong? Or should you keep silent and perhaps feel bad about taking the easy way out? We do not feel that we can offer firm advice on this point. To speak up in such a situation could be very difficult and could invite further ignorant comments. In such a situation, you have to decide on the best strategy to adopt, and often keeping silent might well be the wiser course. If you do keep silent, try not to blame yourself. And if you do speak out and things go wrong, bear in mind that there is no easy answer about how to choose the best course. Such dilemmas indicate the terrible problems that stigma and discrimination can cause. We wrote this book because we wanted to help in a small way to fight ignorance and prejudice, and we hope that in the longer term more enlightened attitudes will prevail. But in the short term the problem is a difficult one.

All the people we have talked about in this book have been troubled, to a greater or lesser extent, by a sense of stigma and discrimination. Jim, as noted above, knew that his uncle had been diagnosed as 'mental' and that this was considered in his family to be a terrible thing. As noted above, he partly explains his own problems by thinking of himself as someone who may be more sensitive or 'spiritual' than other people. Jemma is the most aware of herself as 'a person with a mental illness'. If asked, she will say that her illness is an illness like any other, and that she manages it by taking medication and avoiding stresses that might exacerbate it. However, she is careful about whom she tells about her problems; her manager at work knows, but some of her fellow employees only know that she has a chronic health condition that sometimes causes her to take sick leave. She has a number of supportive friends with whom she can be completely open, and she finds this very helpful.

Loss, depression and anger

Throughout this book, we have tried to offer a message of hope, and to say that being diagnosed with a mental illness is not the end of the world, that there is much that can be done to help sufferers recover and lead full and satisfying lives. Unfortunately, we cannot deny that for many people, the events that surround and follow from such a diagnosis can be very distressing indeed. These can include strange and terrifying experiences of persecution and uncanny events, along with possible conflict with family and friends, trouble with the law, the loss of job, status and relationships and the experience of involuntary treatment and forced confinement. It would be foolish indeed to minimise the negative impact of such events, and some people are haunted by them for many years. Further, for some people these losses cannot be completely put right: a satisfying job or a very close relationship may be lost forever. Such events can lead to a long-term feeling that one's life is not as it could have been.

Unfortunately, this sense of suffering and loss can lead to depression. Such a reaction is natural; no one could be blamed for feeling down at the thought of such losses. Sometimes with depression comes a sense of guilt and self-blame: these dreadful things have happened to me, so somehow I must be responsible. Perhaps I made a wrong decision: I allowed myself to become too stressed, I let my friends talk me into taking those drugs that led to a bad reaction. If it is of any comfort, current thinking, as explained throughout this book, indicates that there is no evidence that schizophrenic experiences can be brought about by an individual's actions alone. Many people have made mistakes in life, or reacted to situations in unhelpful ways, but this does not lead to a schizophrenic illness. Depression, natural as it is, also leads to giving up, which then prevents good things from happening in the future. As we have explained, there are various medical and psychological approaches to depression, but ultimately perhaps the most important treatment for depression is the decision not to lose hope. Good things in the future do not cancel out traumas and losses in the past, but they can put a sense of purpose and fulfilment back into one's life.

Simon has always been troubled by the fact that he was not able to complete his university course. This is partly because his parents had always stressed to him that

Continued

> education was very important, and partly because he had always been a good student in school and taken pride in his ability to do well. For a period of time after his illnesses he tended to brood about the fact that he was 'a failure' and that his life had not amounted to anything. For a period of time he took anti-depressants and found them somewhat helpful. He also discussed the issue of accomplishment with his parents, and they were able to reassure him that his health and happiness were much more important to them than any degree he might earn. As discussed below, Simon also took practical steps to create a sense of accomplishment in his life.

Another reaction to losses can be anger; instead of blaming yourself, you can blame others. Perhaps my parents were not supportive enough, or my spouse was critical and uncaring, or my doctor was insensitive and treated me badly. All these things might be true: parents, friends and doctors are generally no saints, and some of them might be downright bad at what they are doing. A bit of anger in such a circumstance can be perfectly reasonable, as long as it does not stop you from getting on with things. Anger can be dangerous if it leads to brooding over wrongs, or to an attitude that says, 'How can I be expected to accomplish anything with these people against me?' If you have a grievance with someone, it may be a good idea to express it, first to a friend or confidant to get their reaction, and then to the person involved, face to face, in a letter, or in the form of some kind of official complaint. If anger is holding you back from doing things to better your situation, then you are suffering much more than the person with whom you are angry, and that is certainly not helpful. Once again, blame, whether of yourself or someone else, is best kept in proportion; a little may be good, but too much can paralyse you.

What makes life worthwhile?

Having talked about some of the barriers that many sufferers face in trying to live a satisfying life, we turn to what might be the most important question of all: How can I have a worthwhile life? This question applies not just to those who have or are said to have schizophrenia, but to everyone. Before answering this question, it might be worthwhile pointing out a very interesting fact. As noted earlier, schizophrenia is diagnosed all around the world, in rich, developed countries as well as poorer developing ones. Interestingly, sufferers in poor countries, even without many of the medical and psychological treatments described in this book, seem to have a better outcome than in our 'advanced' societies. This might seem puzzling, but there are some points about less developed countries that are probably crucial to understanding such a finding. First, they are generally very family orientated, and often the families are extended into large family groups or clans. In such a society, those who are troubled or handicapped in some way generally receive much more support than people with similar problems in more developed countries. This is not to say that families always know how best to care for their members, but it seems that, on average, the support provided by a large, caring social group is more often helpful than harmful. Further, in less developed economies there is a much greater demand for unskilled labour and in many traditional societies there is little expectation that the average man or woman will 'succeed' or attain a prestigious job. In other words, there are many necessary tasks that people with a variety of problems or handicaps can do, and these jobs are not seen as unimportant or lacking in value.

An example might illustrate this. A few years ago one of the authors went to visit his sister, who used to live in a village in southern Spain. In the village there was a young man known as Paco, who clearly had some sort of disability; he could not speak and behaved very oddly. Nonetheless, everyone in the village seemed to know and accept him. He was given jobs to do and in the evenings, when the men of the village used to congregate and socialise, he was welcomed into the group. Presumably he had always lived in the village and was accepted on that basis. We might wonder if he would have received better or worse care in a large city where no one knew him.

What is the point of this illustration? Almost everyone seems to need two things in his or her life: a supportive social group and some sort of meaningful task or set of tasks to do. The kinds of problems and difficulties discussed in this book may make finding these things more difficult, but we believe that everyone deserves to have these things and has a good chance of finding them.

Tasks and goals

As noted above, our society puts a strong emphasis on achievement and success, and this emphasis can have many problems. In our work as psychologists, we have both seen many people who feel that they are failures because they have failed to reach some specific goal. In some cases, these people appear to everyone else to be very successful: they may have good jobs and nice homes, but they feel that they have not achieved enough. On the other hand, we have seen many other people able to take great satisfaction in what might seem to be relatively modest accomplishments. Human nature is such that anything we strive for and achieve can feel very satisfying. If, for whatever reason, you have lost a good job or failed to achieve some particular distinction, that can be very painful. However, we hope that you will be able to find some new goal to work towards. This goal could be some form of employment, some academic pursuit, some voluntary activity, or a fulfilling hobby. The modern world of work is stressful and demanding, and not everyone can cope with it, but we have already looked in chapter 9 at possible different kinds of work that can be available to those who cannot handle quite as much stress. The most important thing is to have some project underway, even though its realisation might take a long time.

As noted above, Simon always regretted the fact that he never completed university. However, as he began to recover, he looked into various opportunities to develop his academic interests. He had studied history at university, and he began by watching history programmes on television and subscribing to a popular history magazine. Later he found a place in a sheltered work scheme. At first he spent a few hours a week doing a relatively undemanding job, but later he was able to train and to work in a copying shop run by the project. The money that he made was added to his benefit money, and this allowed him to purchase some small luxuries that he previously could not afford. More recently he has started taking a computer course and is saving his money to buy a computer. He eventually plans to take some history courses and he is even thinking of trying to do a history degree part time.

Of course one cannot earn a great deal of money pursuing this sort of work, and unfortunately our society seems to tell us that without a lot of money you cannot be happy. We do not believe that this is the case; we have seen many people take great satisfaction in earning a small amount of money or in accomplishing something that offers no financial reward. If you cannot work, you may have to live on some form of social welfare benefit, something that is sometimes looked down upon. But our society does not actually offer enough highly paid and prestigious jobs so that everyone can have one; there are bound to be people on low pay or living on benefits. If you are receiving benefits, we urge you to get some professional advice on what you are entitled to, and to make sure you receive it. If you are in difficult circumstances and cannot work, a bit of extra money can make a big difference in your quality of life, and we urge you to take what you are entitled to.

Relationships

If a purpose in life is important, so too are relationships. The kinds of experiences discussed throughout this book can put a great strain on relationships, as discussed in the previous chapter. But relationships can be strained by a variety of different experiences and beliefs, such as disagreements about religion or politics. We recall a couple we knew at university who broke up because the woman grew so annoyed about the man's obsession with a particular sports team. Here we offer a simple plea: if possible, do not let differences about beliefs or the possibility of strange experiences disrupt an otherwise good relationship.

When Jim was first ill, he and Rachel would sometimes argue about some of the things he believed in. Once they almost broke up because of an argument they had about a solar eclipse, with Jim maintaining that it proved that the universe had a mystical purpose, and Rachel replying with equal vigour that it proved no such thing. They have now learnt to avoid such arguments and 'agree to disagree'. They will still argue sometimes, but they avoid getting too angry with each other; each has to accept that the other has certain sincerely held beliefs, even though each finds the other's beliefs odd.

Obviously, any serious relationship will have problems sometimes, and every family group will face conflicts. The test of a good relationship is not the absence of conflict but the way it is handled. Unusual experiences and behaviours can be a challenge, but that challenge can be overcome.

The future

We close on one final point: whatever has happened in the past, the future is still open and can be shaped by everyone. We hope that this book has offered some useful ideas to help you shape your future, and has also suggested some sources of help of which you might be able to take advantage. We have seen people confront enormous difficulties and achieve remarkable things in spite of them. Whatever your decision, remember that your future is a precious gift and try to use it wisely. Good luck.

Points covered in this chapter

➡ A diagnosis of serious mental illness can be a source of stigma, but it is best to bear in mind that stigmatising views are the results of ignorance and prejudice.

➡ Guilt, loss, depression and anger are natural reactions to major losses in life, but they do not necessarily prevent one from achieving valuable things.

➡ A sense of achievement and valued relationships are probably the most important things in life and we believe that everyone can attain these things.

➡ We hope that this book will offer you a few suggestions to make positive changes and to improve the future.

Appendix 1: Useful addresses

The intention here is to provide a list of information on organisations that might be helpful if you have a diagnosis of schizophrenia, or you are living with someone with this diagnosis. As we note elsewhere, different groups might benefit different people. It is helpful in the first instance to visit the website of the organisation you might be interested in to find out more information. If, from the information provided there, it looks as though it would be helpful, then you might want to follow this up with a telephone call to find out more. Although we are aware that not everyone has computers, access to the web is increasingly widely available. One useful resource for this in both the UK and the US is local libraries most of which now offer a number of terminals with internet access. Organisations are listed under three headings: General information; Volunteering organisations; and Self-help organisations. Within each section organisations are listed alphabetically. It was not our intention to give any one organisation prominence over any other, merely to present information for the reader to review.

General information

Association for Supported Employment
Huw Davies (Chair)
Bury EST
24 Ribchester Drive
Bury BL9 9JT
Tel: 0161 253 6588
Fax: 0161 253 6504
Mob: 07946 537286
Email: huw@buryest.org.uk
Internet: www.afse.org.uk

Association for Supported Employment is a national group in the UK representing approximately two hundred supported employment agencies. It aims to develop provision of supported and valued employment, with associated training opportunities. In addition to helping members with setting up and developing these opportunities, it sees itself as having an important liaison role with national government in respect of these issues.

Jobcentre Plus Secretariat
Level 6
Caxton House
Tothill Street
London
SW1H 9NA
Internet: www.jobplus.gov.uk

Job Centre Plus programme is intended to help people into employment and training. Those areas that have a Job Centre Plus offer personal advisers to help individuals work their way through the complications of finding appropriate employment in the context of their other needs. There are currently approximately 140 of these centres across the UK at present, with targets for coverage of all UK towns by 2006.

Mental Health Act Commission
Maid Marian House
56 Hounds Gate
Nottingham
NG1 6BG
Tel: 0115 943 7100
Fax: 0115 943 7101
Email: ChiefExec@mhac.trent.nhs.uk
Internet: www.mhac.trent.nhs.uk/Commission.htm

On its website, the Mental Health Act Commission defines its role as follows: 'The Mental Health Act Commission was established in 1983 and consists of some 170 members (Commissioners), including laypersons, lawyers, doctors, nurses, social workers, psychologists and other specialists.'

Its functions include, among others:

1. reviewing how the Mental Health Act (1983) works;
2. visiting patients detained under the Act in hospitals and mental nursing homes;
3. investigating complaints that fall within the Commission's remit;
4. the appointment of medical practitioners and others to give second opinions in cases where this is required by the Act.

The National Association of Citizens Advice Bureaux
Myddelton House
115–123 Pentonville Road
London
N1 9LZ
Tel: 0207 833 02181
Internet: www.nacab.org.uk

The Citizens Advice Bureaux are registered charities that provide free, confidential advice. There are Citizens Advice Bureaux in most towns and cities across the UK. Their website currently lists

2231 Bureaux, so if you live in the UK there should be one near you. The Citizens Advice Bureau advisors deal with debt issues, benefits, housing, legal matters and employment. Advisers can help fill out forms, write letters, negotiate with creditors and represent clients at court or tribunal. This role includes, but is not unique to, people with mental health problems.

US Department of Labor
Frances Perkins Building
200 Constitution Avenue, NW
Washington, DC 20210
Tel: 1-866-4-USA-DOL
Internet: www.dol.gov

The US Department of Labor provides information on Labor Offices for each State. Contact information for each Labor Office is also to be found on the Department of Labor website.

Volunteering organisations

Do It Yourself
1211 N LaSalle Drive, Suite 1603
Chicago, IL 60610-8010
Internet: www.CharityGuide.org

This Internet-based guide was developed by a web entrepreneur and provides information on a wide range of volunteering opportunities. These range from volunteer activity that can be done briefly from home using a home computer to more detailed information on joining in the activities of major charities.

National Association for Volunteer Bureaux
New Oxford House
16 Waterloo Street
Birmingham

B2 5UG
Tel: 0121 633 4555
Internet: www.navb.org.uk

Volunteer Bureaux (VB) are part of Volunteer Development England. There are more than 350 Volunteer Bureaux in the UK. They may also be listed locally as Volunteer Centres, Councils for Voluntary Service, Voluntary Action or Volunteer Development Agencies. Their role is to provide information and advice concerning the range and availability of voluntary work for people in their local area.

TimeBank
The Mezzanine
Elizabeth House
39 York Road
London
SE1 7NQ
Tel: 0207 401 5420
Fax: 0207 401 5421
Internet: www.timebank.org.uk

TimeBank was developed out of the success of Comic Relief. The TimeBank website contains information on a wide range of possibilities for people interested in volunteering large or small amounts of time. TimeBank has links with other volunteering organisations across the UK, which include Volunteer Bureaux, referred to above.

Self-help organisations

Britain

The Hearing Voices Network
91 Oldham Street
Manchester

M4 1LW
Tel: 0161 834 5768
Email: hearingvoices@care4free.net
Internet: www.hearing-voices.org.uk

The Hearing Voices Network was first established in 1988 in Manchester. It is a group run by voices-hearers, with an increasing number of local groups across the UK and beyond. The Network provides information and support to people who hear voices, irrespective of whether they have a formal psychiatric history. The Network has also become involved in training for users, volunteers and professionals.

Making Space
46 Allen Street
Warrington
WA2 7JB
Tel: 01925 571680
Internet: www.makingspace.co.uk

Making Space runs forty self-help groups throughout the north of England. It also provides family support workers and befrienders to people with a diagnosis of schizophrenia or associated mental health problems. They also provide supported accommodation and support for people re-entering education or employment.

The Mental Health Foundation
83 Victoria Street
London
SW1H 0HW
Tel: 0207 802 0300
Fax: 0207 802 0301
Email: mhf@mhf.org.uk
Internet: www.mentalhealth.org.uk

This is a large mental health charity which aims to promote good practise in working with people with mental health problems. It is involved in provision of information and training. It also has a number of initiatives in clinical research, including a large programme of user-led research.

MIND
15–19 Broadway
London
E15 4BQ
Email: contact@mind.org.uk
Internet: www.mind.org.uk

MIND is a registered charity with over 210 local MIND associations across the UK. These local associations provide advice, support and information to people with mental health problems. MIND also produce publications covering a wide range of mental health and related issues. It is also a campaigning organisation which aims to promote the rights and improve the quality of life of people with a mental health history.

ReThink
Head Office
30 Tabernacle Street
London
EC2A 4DD
Tel: 0845 456 0455 (general enquiries)
National Advice Line: 0208 974 6814 (open 10am to 3pm, M–F)
Email: advice@rethink.org; info@rethink.org
Internet: www.rethink.org

ReThink is the new name for what was previously called the 'National Schizophrenia Fellowship'. It is a large organisation, employing over 1800 staff across the UK. ReThink sets out to provide a range of services for people with schizophrenia and their families. These services include: employment projects, supported housing, day services, helplines, residential care and respite centres. Like other organisations, ReThink also acts as a campaigning organisation for people with mental health problems and their relatives.

SANE
1st Floor, Cityside House
40 Adler Street
London, E1 1EE
Tel: 0207 375 1002
SANELINE: 0845 767 8000 (open from 12 noon until 2am, every day of the year)
Internet: www.sane.org.uk

SANE provides a helpline for anyone with mental health problems. It also exists to provide information and emotional support to caregivers. In addition, SANE aims to facilitate better training and education to ensure better services for people with mental health problems. It is also involved in supporting clinical research.

Survivors Network
Ms Julia Bromley (Survivors Network Co-ordinator)
Survivors Network
c/o Voluntary Action Manchester
North Square
11–13 Spear Street
Manchester M1 1JU
Internet: www.healthy-life-styles.com

The stated aims of the Survivors Network, according to its website, are:

Developing, sharing, and promoting creative and innovative good practise in mental health recovery, locally, nationally, and internationally. Improving the information, education, and support available to people who experience mental distress to assist them in their recovery to lead more fulfilling lives. Building mutually beneficial partnerships with mental health professionals and other agencies to ensure that the recovery vision remains at the heart of mental health service development via information, education, training, research, policy work, consultancy and volunteering. Supporting and promoting our own and other recovery related initiatives, locally, nationally, and internationally.

United States

National Alliance for the Mentally Ill (NAMI)
Colonial Place Three
2107 Wilson Boulevard, Suite 300
Arlington, VA 22201-3042
Tel: +1 (703) 524 7600
Fax: +1 (703) 524 9094
TDD: +1 (703) 516 7227
Member Services: +1 (888) 999 NAMI
Information and Services: +1 (800) 950 NAMI
Internet: www.nami.org

NAMI is a 'nonprofit, grassroots, self-help, support and advocacy organization of consumers, families, and friends of people with severe mental illnesses'.

It has more than one thousand local affiliates and fifty state organisations in the US which aim to provide education and support. They also provide practical support and information on financial, job, housing and health issues.

National Mental Health Consumers' Self-Help Clearing House
1211 Chestnut Street, Suite 1207
Philadelphia, PA 19107
Tel: (800) 553–4KEY [4539] or (215) 751–1810
Fax: (215) 636–6312
Email: info@mhselfhelp.org

The Clearing House provides assistance to self-help/advocacy groups and individual consumers. It also helps network consumer groups, individual consumers, and advocacy groups from around the US.

Schizophrenics Anonymous/National Schizophrenia Foundation
403 Seymour Avenue, Suite 202
Lansing, MI 48933
Tel: +1 (517) 485 7168
Fax: +1 (517) 485 7180
Consumer Line: +1 (800) 482 9534
Email: inquiries@nsfoundation.org (general questions);
litrequest@nsfoundation.org (literature request);
sareferrals@nsfoundation.org (Schizophrenics Anonymous Group Referral)
Internet: www.sanonymous.org or www.nsfoundation.org

Schizophrenics Anonymous is a self-help group. There are over 150 groups across the US and elsewhere. It is a user-run and led organisation that aims to provide support for people with schizophrenia, in order to help facilitate active involvement of individuals in taking steps towards their own recovery. This works in partnership with the National Schizophrenia Foundation, which is a national US non-profit agency working to deliver self-help support and to increase public understanding of schizophrenia and related issues.

Canada

Schizophrenia Society of Canada
50 Acadia Avenue – Suite 205
Markham, ON
L3R 0B3
Tel: (905) 415-2007
Fax: (905) 415-2337
Email: info@schizophrenia.ca

The Schizophrenia Society of Canada (SSC) is a national registered charity. SSC works with ten provincial societies and their over one hundred chapters/branches to alleviate the suffering caused by schizophrenia and related mental disorders. To this end, SSC and its provincial affiliates carry out public awareness and education, family support, advocacy and research-funding initiatives and programmes.

World Fellowship for Schizophrenia and Allied Disorders
124 Merton Street, Suite 507
Toronto, Ontario M4S 2Z2
Canada
Tel: +1 (416) 961 2855
Fax: +1 (416) 961 1948
Internet: www.world-schizophrenia.org

The World Fellowship for Schizophrenia and Allied Disorders (WFSAD) is an international group of twenty-two national organisations and fifty smaller groups. WFSAD supports and facilitates the work of these groups. It aims to increase knowledge about schizophrenia and explicitly acknowledges the importance of both social and medical support. It is a charity recognised by the Canadian government.

Other websites

SANE, Australia: www.sane.org

Schizophrenia Fellowship of New South Wales:
www.sfnsw.webcentral.com.au

Mental Illness Fellowship of South Australia, Inc.:
www.sfsa.asn.au

Schizophrenia Ireland: www.sirl.ie

Appendix 2: Relaxation methods

Deep muscle relaxation

First we offer an example of deep muscle relaxation. Deep muscle relaxation was developed in the 1930s and has been shown in many studies to be a safe and effective form of relaxation. It is based on the idea that many people do not actually know how to recognise a relaxing state, and its goal is to teach people how to relax all their muscles. This particular script was one used by Jim; in particular, the relaxing scene at the end was one that he thought would be particularly soothing for him. However, if you would like to try it, please feel free to change the ending and to focus on a scene that you would find particularly soothing and peaceful.

If you wish to use this script, you need a comfortable chair and a quiet room. You can record these words on an audio cassette or ask a friend with a soothing voice to do it for you. The person recording should speak in a slow, calming tone, and can repeat parts of the tape several times in a relaxing manner if you find this helpful. Relaxation is an acquired skill; if you find that the tape is not that relaxing at first, we suggest that you practise it several times. The goal is to pay attention to the feelings of tension and relaxation in the varying muscle groups and gradually learn how relaxation feels, which can then help you learn how to make your muscles more and more relaxed. Finally, as noted above, we include the scene that Jim suggested to his therapist when the tape was made. He imagined himself coming home from a party late at night and sitting in a local park, and he thought that the cool night air, the play of the street lights on the trees and the stars high above were all images that he found especially relaxing. If you do not find this scene relaxing, you can imagine and describe another one that you personally find more suitable.

I'd like you to close your eyes, sit comfortably and relax. If there's any tension anywhere in your body, just let it relax away. Your body should be very loose and limp and relaxed, very loose and limp and relaxed. Just let yourself relax. Good. Now I'd like you to tense your right hand. Just make a fist with your right hand. I'd like you to feel all the feelings of tension in your right hand. Just feel how that feels. Good. Now, relax, relax. Just let your right hand relax. Just feel the feelings of relaxation in your right hand. Just feel how that feels. Your right hand is very loose, and limp and relaxed, very loose and limp and relaxed. Good.

Now I'd like you to tense your left hand. Just make a fist with your left hand. I'd like you to feel all the feelings of tension in your left hand. Just feel how that feels. Good. Now, relax, relax. Just let your left hand relax. Just feel the feelings of relaxation in your left hand. Just feel how that feels. Your left hand is very loose, and limp and relaxed, very loose and limp and relaxed. Good.

Now I'd like you to tense up your right upper arm. You can do this by touching your right shoulder with your right hand

and making your arm very tense. Try to feel all the feelings of tension in your right arm. Try to feel how that feels. Now, relax, relax. Just let your right arm relax. Just feel the feelings of relaxation in your right arm. Just feel how that feels. Your right arm and right hand are very loose, and limp and relaxed, very loose and limp and relaxed. Good.

Now I'd like you to tense up your left upper arm. You can do this by touching your left shoulder with your left hand and making your arm very tense. Try to feel all the feelings of tension in your left arm. Try to feel how that feels. Now, relax, relax. Just let your left arm relax. Just feel the feelings of relaxation in your left arm. Just feel how that feels. Your left arm and left hand are very loose, and limp and relaxed, very loose and limp and relaxed. Good.

Now I'd like you to tense up your shoulders. Shrug up your shoulders towards your ears. Your shoulders are very tense, try to feel all the feelings of tension in your shoulders. Try to feel how that feels. Good. Now, relax, relax. Just let your shoulders relax. Your shoulders should be very loose and limp and relaxed, very loose and limp and relaxed, your shoulders and arms should be very loose and limp and relaxed, very loose and limp and relaxed. Good.

Now I'd like you to relax your neck. Just gently let your head role from side to side. Don't do this too vigorously, but just gently rotate your neck back and forth and let all those muscles relax. Just let your whole upper body relax. You should feel very loose and limp and relaxed, very loose and limp and relaxed. Good.

Now take a deep breath. Hold it (pause about one second) and now let it out. And as you let it out, you feel all the tension leaving your body. You feel very loose and limp and relaxed, very loose and limp and relaxed. Good.

Now tense up your right foot. You can do this by curling up your toes. Just feel all the tension in your right foot. Try to feel how that feels. And now, relax, relax. Just let your right foot relax. Your right foot should be very loose and limp and relaxed, very loose and limp and relaxed. Try to feel how that feels. Good.

Now tense up your left foot. You can do this by curling up your toes. Just feel all the tension in your left foot. Try to feel how that feels. And now, relax, relax. Just let your left foot relax. Your left foot should be very loose and limp and relaxed, very loose and limp and relaxed. Try to feel how that feels. Good.

Now tense up your right leg. Just press down hard with your right heel and tense up your right leg. Try to feel all the tension in your right leg. Try to feel how that feels. And now, relax, relax. Just let your right leg relax. Your right leg and your right foot should be very loose and limp and relaxed, very loose and limp and relaxed. Try to feel how that feels. Good.

Now tense up your left leg. Just press down hard with your left heel and tense up your left leg. Try to feel all the tension in your left leg. Try to feel how that feels. And now, relax. Just let your left leg relax. Your left leg and your left foot should be very loose and limp and relaxed. Both your legs and both your feet should be very loose and limp and relaxed, very loose and limp and relaxed. Try to feel how that feels. Good.

Now tense up your stomach. Tighten up all the muscles in your stomach. Try to feel all the tension in your stomach, try to feel how that feels. Now, relax, relax. Just let your stomach relax. Your stomach should be very loose and limp and relaxed, very loose and limp and relaxed. Your whole lower body should be very loose and limp and relaxed. Try to feel all the feelings of relaxation in your lower body, try to feel how that feels. Good.

Now take a deep breath. Hold it (pause about one second) and now let it out. And as you let it out, you feel all the tension leaving your body. You feel very loose and limp and relaxed, very loose and limp and relaxed. Good.

Now tense up all the muscles of your forehead. Just wrinkle up your forehead, try to feel all the tension in your forehead, try to feel how that feels. And now, relax, relax. Just let your forehead relax. Your forehead should be very loose and limp and relaxed, very loose and limp and relaxed. Good.

Now tense up your eyes. Squeeze your eyes tight shut, try to feel all the tension in your eyes. And now, relax, relax. Just let your eyes relax. Your eyes should feel very loose and limp and relaxed, very loose and limp and relaxed. Try to feel how that feels. Good.

Now tense up your nose. Wrinkle up your nose, try to feel all the tension in your nose. And now, relax, relax. Just let your nose relax. Your nose should feel very loose and limp and relaxed, very loose and limp and relaxed. Try to feel how that feels. Good.

Now tense up your cheeks. Pull back your cheeks in a wide grin, try to feel all the tension in your cheeks. And now, relax, relax. Just let your cheeks relax. Your cheeks should feel very loose and limp and relaxed, very loose and limp and relaxed. Try to feel how that feels. Good.

Now finally, tense up your jaw. Clench your teeth, and try to feel all the tension in your jaw. And now, relax, relax. Just let your jaw relax. Your jaw should feel very loose and limp and relaxed, very loose and limp and relaxed. Try to feel how that feels. Good.

Now take a deep breath. Hold it (pause about one second) and now let it out. And as you let it out, you feel all the tension leaving your body. You feel very loose and limp and relaxed, very loose and limp and relaxed. Good.

Now I'm going to count from one to five, and as I do you are going to feel more and more relaxed. If there's any tension anywhere in your body, just let it relax away. One. Relax, relax. Two. You feel very loose and limp and relaxed, very loose and limp and relaxed. Three. Just let all the tension leave your body, your body feels very limp, as if you have no bones at all. Four. Relax, relax. You feel very loose and limp and relaxed, very loose and limp and relaxed. Five.

Now you feel very relaxed and very comfortable. If there's any tension anywhere in your body, just let it relax away. Just imagine that you are sitting in the middle of the park on a warm summer night. You're sitting with your back against a tree. You're all alone, it's all very quiet and peaceful. It's so late at night that there are no cars, no people, everything is deserted. There's a cool, pleasant breeze, and you can hear the leaves of the trees gently rustling. You can see the lights of the street lamps on the leaves, but otherwise the park is dark and silent, there's nobody there. You feel pleasantly tired, just relaxed, with nothing to do. You're just lying with your back against the tree, feeling very comfortable. You look up and see the moon, high up in the sky, lighting up the clouds, and you see a few stars twinkling. It's all very peaceful, and you feel very relaxed and comfortable. You have nowhere to go, nothing to do, you feel very relaxed, just watching the clouds drift across the moon and the leaves gently swaying in the breeze. You feel very comfortable, and very loose and limp and relaxed. Now you can just lie here for as long as you want, feeling very loose and limp and relaxed, very loose and limp and relaxed, very loose and limp and relaxed.

Mindfulness relaxation

This approach was used by Jemma, referred to in chapter 7 (Cognitive Behavioural Therapy). She had tried the deep muscle relaxation approach, but it did not work for her. She wanted to try another approach and liked the idea of the mindfulness approach when it was discussed with her. There is a large literature about the nature of mindfulness and the links between mindfulness and eastern religion and philosophy. Such discussions are beyond the scope of this book. If the reader is interested in exploring this approach in more detail a reference is provided at the end of this section. In clinical practice we have found that the simple application of the breathing approach described below is often helpful for people who find deep muscle relaxation too involved.

Many people find that most of the time their attention is focused in the past and the future more than in the present. This is particularly true when you are tired, stressed or worried. The thoughts that make you feel this way are generally about what you fear may happen, what the consequences may be and whether you will cope. The problem with this future thinking is that we cannot usually visualise the future with any great accuracy and therefore expend large amounts of energy trying to solve problems that will actually turn out to be different when we have to deal with them in the present. The cost of this thinking is often that it makes us feel worse and saps our energy, actually making it harder to deal with the challenges that face us.

You may yourself be aware that when you are talking to one person you are already thinking about what you need to do afterwards. Similarly many people who drive have had the experience of being so wrapped up in their thoughts about what they will do when they get to their destination, that they have barely even noticed the route they have driven. Mindfulness is the process of becoming more aware of where you are 'in the present'. This is often helpful for people as they are then free to deal with situations as they actually are, rather than as they might become or have previously been. I am going to describe a breathing exercise that is used to aid mindfulness. Before I do this, there are a number of points to bear in mind:

1. To practise this breathing exercise, find a quiet place that is not too brightly lit. Try to make sure that you will not be

disturbed when you are doing the exercise. Turn off any television or radio in the room and switch off your telephone.

2. When you are doing the breathing exercise your only task is to notice your breathing and the sensations associated with it. This might include the feel of the air coming in and out, the feel of the movement of muscles and the feel of your stomach moving as you breathe.

3. Paying attention to your breathing means only that. You are not to consciously try to change your breath or make yourself relax.

4. You do not need to think about your breathing, rather that you should be aware of it and notice the sensations associated with it.

5. It is best to use diaphragmatic breathing for this exercise. To do this, put your hand on your stomach and feel as you try to push your stomach out when you breathe in and in when you breathe out. It can take a little time to get comfortable with this type of breathing, so practise it a few times now before the exercise begins.

6. Once you are comfortable with diaphragmatic breathing you are ready to start the mindfulness exercise. This will last fifteen minutes and when the time is up you will be asked to open your eyes and refocus on your surroundings. You will be given some brief instructions and then after that the guide will not speak unless this is necessary for the rest of the exercise.

Mindfulness exercise

1. Find a comfortable sitting position with your spine straight and let your shoulders drop.
2. Close your eyes.
3. Bring your attention to your stomach, feeling it rise or expand gently on the inbreath and fall or recede on the outbreath.

4. Keep focusing on your breathing, 'being with' each inbreath for its full duration and with each outbreath for its full duration, as if riding the waves of your own breathing.

5. Every time you notice that your mind has wandered off the breath, notice what it was that took you away and then gently bring your attention back to your stomach and the feeling of breath coming in and out.

6. If your mind wanders away from the breath a thousand times, then your 'job' is simply to bring it back to the breath every time, no matter what it becomes preoccupied with.

7. Notice what it feels like to spend time just being with your breath without having to do anything.

8. At this point people often find that they like to visualise a pleasant scene while they let their breath come and go. If you wish to do this, try to think of a time and place when you felt calm, warm and secure. If this is hard try to picture an ideal scene, e.g. in a quiet countryside setting, by a gentle river or on a beach in the sunshine.

9. When fifteen minutes have elapsed, open your eyes and gently re-orientate yourself to your surroundings. Be aware of the sensation of being 'in the present'. Try to notice this sensation as you go about your daily activities.

Reference

Kabat-Zinn, J. 1990. *Full Catastrophe Living: Using the wisdom of your body and mind to face stress, pain, and illness.* New York, Dell Publishing

Further Reading

Anthony, W. A. 1993. 'Recovery from Mental Illness: the guiding vision of the mental health service system in the 1990s'. *Psychosocial Rehabilitation Journal* 16(4), 11–23

Birchwood, M. and Jackson, C. 2001. *Schizophrenia.* Hove, UK, Psychology Press

Blackman, L. 2001. *Hearing Voices: Contesting the Voice of Reason.* London, Free Association Books

Chadwick, P. 1997. *Schizophrenia: In Search of Dignity for People with Schizophrenia.* Hove, UK, Bruner–Routledge

Coleman, R. and Smith, M. 1997. *Working with Voices.* Gloucester, UK, Handsell Publishing

May, R. 2000. Extract from: *Recent Advances in Understanding Mental Illness and Psychotic Experiences.* A report by the British Psychological Society, Division of Clinical Psychology. Available free from www.bps.org.uk/sub-syst/dcp/publications.cfm

Mueser, K. T. and Gungerich, S. 1994. *Coping with Schizophrenia: A Guide for Families.* Oakland, CA, New Harbinger

National Institute of Clinical Excellence. 2003. *Treating and Managing Schizophrenia: Understanding NICE Guidance – Information for People with Schizophrenia, Their Advocates and Carers.* London, NICE

Romme, M. and Escher, S. 1993. *Accepting Voices.* London, MIND

Torrey, F. E. 2001. *Surviving Schizophrenia.* New York, HarperCollins

Turner, T. 2003. *Schizophrenia: Your Questions Answered.* London, Churchill–Livingstone

Index